ANNE PHILLIPS was born in Lancaster in 1950. She studied Philosophy and Politics at the University of Bristol from 1968-71 and went on to take an M.Sc. in West African Politics at the School of Oriental and African Studies. In 1982 she was awarded a Ph.D. from the City University for her work on colonial policy in British West Africa. Since 1975 she has been a lecturer in politics at the City of London Polytechnic and, as part of her work, teaches a course on feminist politics in Britain through the nineteenth and twentieth centuries. She has been active in the women's movement for many years and has written widely in feminist and socialist journals, particularly on the subject of the connection between feminist and socialist politics which is central to *Divided Loyalties*. Anne Phillips is the author of *Hidden Hands: Women and Economic Policies* (1983). She lives in London.

DIVIDED
LOYALTIES

Dilemmas of Sex and Class

Anne Phillips

Published by VIRAGO PRESS Limited 1987
41 William IV Street, London WC2N 4DB

Copyright © Anne Phillips 1987

British Library Cataloguing in Publication Data

Phillips, Anne, *1950-*
    Divided loyalties.
    1. Women—Social conditions
    I. Title
    305.4′2   HQ1206

    ISBN 0-86068-553-5

Typeset in North Wales by
Derek Doyle & Associates, Mold, Clwyd
Printed and bound in Great Britain by
Cox & Wyman Ltd, Reading

Contents

Acknowledgements

I have been much helped in writing this book by those who read and commented on early drafts and those who in the course of discussion have pushed me to develop my ideas: I need hardly say that none of these is thereby implicated in the result. My thanks then to Sally Alexander, Sarah Benton, Irene Bruegel, Hermione Harris, Sue Himmelweit, Cora Kaplan, Jean McCrindle, Mary McIntosh, Ann Pettifor, Eileen Phillips, Barbara Taylor. I am particularly grateful to Michèle Barrett and Cynthia Cockburn, both of whom volunteered to read the entire first draft, and whose comments were perceptive and precise; and to Lynne Segal, who not only shared her ideas and concerns, but conveyed a (probably misplaced) confidence in me that was always a source of strength. My editors at Virago were also encouraging and full of suggestions: thanks to Ursula Owen for prompting me to embark on the project and to Ruthie Petrie for putting me on the right lines to finish. Special thanks to Ciaran Driver, who neither typed my manuscript nor ironed my shirts, but who worked so hard himself he persuaded me to do the same; much love but no thanks to Declan, whose arrival set back the book by a year.

1 Liberation for All or Just for a Few?

Feminism has long been described and dismissed as a middle-class affair, a movement that talks in the name of all women, but pursues the narrower concerns of those more privileged ones. The accusation is meant as a deterrent, for when a movement lays claims to radical intent, the wrong class can shake its pretensions. For left politics in particular, 'middle class' has long been a term of abuse, and while exceptions have been worthy and frequent, many socialists in the nineteenth and twentieth centuries have justified their distance from the women's movement in terms of what they saw as its middle-class nature. More curious is the way the same complaint has surfaced in less radical circles, for those who in other contexts quite happily deride class as an old-fashioned notion (the working class, they may say, no longer exists; class politics itself has languished and died) can still turn with relief to the middle-class taint. You may like the middle class, you might be one of them yourself, but the accusation is all too attractive. In British politics at least, if you want to cast doubt on a movement's credibility – and the object of discussion might be the women's movement, it might be the Labour Party, it might be any of a number of campaigns around the siting of a motorway, an airport, a nuclear power station – if you want to discredit its supporters, you identify them as middle-class folk. The effect it seems is instantaneous: their pretensions are undermined.

As far as the women's movement is concerned, the

preponderance of middle-class women among its supporters has been widely accepted even by those sympathetic to its aims, and it is 'bourgeois' women who are usually credited with the first stirrings of discontent. In Britain, some of the earliest voices to be raised were in the seventeenth century, and Juliet Mitchell has argued that the history of feminism ran in parallel with the history of the concept of equality, and that both came to the fore at that brief moment when the bourgeoisie could claim for itself a revolutionary and progressive role.

> Feminism as a conscious, that is self-conscious, protest movement, arose as part of the revolutionary bourgeois tradition that had equality of mankind as its highest goal. The first expressions of feminism were endowed with the strengths of the concept of equality and circumscribed by its limitations. Feminism arose in England in the seventeenth century as a conglomeration of precepts and a series of demands by women who saw themselves as a distinct sociological group and one that was completely excluded from the tenets and principles of the new society. The seventeenth-century feminists were mainly middle-class women who argued their case in explicit relation to the massive change in society that came about with the end of feudalism and the beginning of capitalism. As the new bourgeois man held up the torch against absolutist tyranny and argued for freedom and equality, the new bourgeois woman wondered why she was being left out.[1]

The equality espoused by these movements was what we would call 'formal' as opposed to real equality: the right to equal treatment before the law regardless of one's birth or station; the triple rights, in John Locke's phrase, to 'life, liberty and property'. As the centuries progressed, further more specific rights were added to the feminist list: the right to education, to a vote, to professional employment, to hold property in one's own and not one's husband's name. By the nineteenth century women were clearly on the move, but as they began to organise their feminist campaigns, the preponderance of middle-class women was noted both then and now. Explaining this in *Faces of Feminism*, Olive Banks has argued that it was the separation of work from home that was one of the key structural changes to give rise to an organised movement; this separation, she suggested, affected 'both middle-class and working-class women, but it affected them differently, and it was amongst the middle classes that dissatisfaction turned into the kind of channel that produced the feminist movement'.[2] In *The Petticoat Rebellion*, Marion Ramelson argued that 'the essence of the demand for women's rights in every field of human endeavour is for women to have rights already enjoyed by men'; it follows, she suggested, that women can only push their own interests after the men in their lives have won their own. And as long as working men were 'economically, politically and socially a crabbed and confined part of the nation', working women could not be feminists; the task of formulating the demands had to devolve onto middle-class women.[3]

The analysis is partly about the constituency from which the movement drew its supporters, but it is also about what has long been part of the feminist tradition: its appeal to equality of rights. As Michèle Barrett has recently commented, the 'dominant traditions of feminism are couched in terms of morality, justice or equal rights', relying 'on a notion of the self-evident fairness of distributing rights and opportunities equally among humans'.[4] Born out of a period when women lacked the most basic of political rights, the new women's movement inevitably highlighted political emancipation – equal rights to all of us as equal citizens of society. Yet equal rights as we know can be a limited demand: equality in principle is not the same as equality in practice. The equal right to a vote is now conceded – not just for men of all conditions but for women too – but it has not guaranteed equal access to power. The equal right to education has been established as a principle, but schools in working-class neighbourhoods are under-resourced, and girls are taught differently from boys. The equal right to a job is no longer legally contested, but black men and black and white women still get a raw deal. If feminism is essentially about equal rights with men rather than equal existence, what relevance will it have for those at the bottom of the pile? A recent journalistic account of women students at Oxford noted that by their own account, all were feminists now; and since the same report took pains to show how little student radicalism touched their lives, what sense does this give us of what feminism can mean?

When the contemporary women's movement exploded into new life in the late 1960s, many of us were ignorant of the history of women's struggles – but we still felt we knew enough to claim our own movement as more broadly based than before. Activists from earlier generations seemed a strange and alien breed: when Sheila Rowbotham was growing up she thought of feminists as 'shadowy figures in old-fashioned clothes who were somehow connected with headmistresses who said you shouldn't wear high heels and make-up ... frightening people in tweed suits and horn-rimmed glasses with stern buns at the backs of their heads.'[5] Further back into the previous century, the feminists seemed a pretty dull lot: not so much radical visionaries as sensible reformers, and concentrated (as we thought) among the higher echelons of the middle class; women whose sense of subordination was heightened by the contrast with powerful husbands or brothers; whose chosen way forward was through the privileged path of university and the professions. Working-class women, we were taught to believe, were either absent from politics or engaged in other concerns.

If these were indeed our predecessors, they seemed confined by limited aims: just a few reforms here and there; just a moderate improvement in the status of women. The campaign for the vote was apparently central to their preoccupations, and knowing this, we could bask in a superior glow. No one could have fooled *us* that the vote would make such a difference. From what we knew of nineteenth-century feminism, its calls to action echoed back as the concerns of an already favoured middle class. From our vantage point in the exuberant sixties and seventies, we could feel ourselves immensely more ambitious. The feminism of our generation would challenge everything, far exceeding the moderate demands of 'bourgeois' reform.

Yet our own credentials were soon brought into question, as we in turn were identified as middle class: a categorisation that now rested less on money and more on education. Frankie Rickford has described the women who made up the new movement in the late 1960s and early 1970s as 'higher educated heterosexual white women in their mid-twenties to thirties';[6] in much the same terms David Bouchier identifies them as 'mainly young – between 20 and 35 years old – mainly university graduates or students and almost without exception already active in politics'.[7] Beneficiaries of the 1944 Education Act and indeed of the whole post-war expansion of the welfare state, the new feminists seemed paradigms of upward mobility. We may not have had private incomes, and our parents were hardly well off, but the jobs we could aspire to set us apart from the more dreary statistics of women's work. If such were and are the typical feminists, what right had they to speak for women?

What hope has the movement of broader appeal?

This of course is what critics have seized on, arguing that the class character of feminism is no accident, that the issues of sexual equality will appeal only to those who are already on their way. The 'ordinary' woman, it is said, will have no truck with women's liberation; she cannot luxuriate in moans about male dominance; she has quite enough on her plate as it is. 'Equal pay and opportunities' rings hollow when her husband earns so little. 'Why be a wife?' is a meaningless query when the alternatives remain so bleak. Feminism, it is argued, is the prerogative of the more privileged woman – she who has benefitted from a college education, who has the earning power to strike out on her own, who is comfortable enough in her material conditions to turn her attention to the 'trivia' of sexual roles. Those less privileged may have their complaints against men, but their energies are consumed in more pressing – and, it is implied, less selfish – concerns.

Through much of the 1970s, feminists did their battle with such put-downs. We were irritated by the implication that middle-class women had no real problems of their own, as if only by sliding our oppression under the more acceptable cloak of class could we hope to make out a case. We were infuriated by the parrot-like insistence that the Women's Liberation Movement was unrepresentative; delighted perhaps with what we were learning of the hidden history of working-class feminism; impatient of those who were less well-informed. We rejected the patronising assumption that working-class women were innocently content; refused the loaded priorities (so much loved by our socialist friends) of workers first and women second; noted by-the-by that not all workers are men. Class, we argued, must be shifted from the centre of the stage, for its language has denied the experience of women.

But as the critics from without came to be joined by critics from within, the response has been less easy. The women's movement itself is now arguably in crisis, and since the late 1970s has been increasingly – often bitterly – divided along the fault lines of sexuality, race and class; today it may be wishful thinking to talk of a women's 'movement' at all. That feminists should disagree is not a new phenomenon, but our divisions now seem peculiarly fraught, our anger turned in on ourselves. The women's movement has changed in both emphasis and constituency, and when Frankie Rickford identified the centrality of white middle-class women to the early years of the movement, it was to counterpose this to what she saw as a later radical departure.

> Since this wave of feminism began fifteen years or so ago it
> has undergone profound change. The old way of doing things
> – consciousness raising on Monday night and campaigning
> on Thursday and Friday – has given way to action-based
> groups in which learning to dare to act is an explicit part of
> the exercise. The movement's social base no longer consists
> of higher educated heterosexual white women in their mid
> twenties to thirties as it did in the sixties and seventies. Now
> many more very young, working-class and black women are
> feminist activists and lots are lesbians.[8]

The new triad of heterosexism, racism and classism which this
account hints at has generated considerable heat, with the debate
around racism the most prominent and troubled. Feminists have
proved no more immune to racism than the society they inhabit,
and as they have documented this, black women have challenged
many of the preoccupations of the contemporary women's
movement. They have pointed to the stereotypical perceptions of
Asian women as passive, of Afro-Caribbean men as peculiarly
sexist. They have demonstrated how many of the movement's
demands – around the family or abortion or sexuality or work –
have been premised on the experience of white women alone. They
have argued convincingly for an analysis that will integrate the
complex dynamics of gender and race and class, one that will that
acknowledge the centrality of race in the experience of black
women.[9]

The parallels with the feminist critique of men and sexism are too
obvious to be ignored, and white feminists who cut their teeth on
arguments against 'men both stereotyping women and also
assuming that their arguments about men apply to women, often
with completely contradictory consequences for their arguments
taken as a whole',[10] cannot in good faith refuse to listen when black
feminists turn the same arguments against their own previous
practice. My own work, to take one example, has focussed on
part-time employment as a defining experience of women in Britain
today and highlighted this as a crucial area for action.[11] Only
belatedly did I even notice that this was the experience of *white*
women, and not of women as a whole, and while the discovery does
not of itself discredit the importance of part-time employment, it
does raise questions as to my assumptions about women. With all

our knowledge of the ways that 'man' has masqueraded for both the sexes, white feminists have not proved equally alert to the ways that 'women' has covered for black and white alike – and this is a powerful indictment.

Related arguments have emerged over the privileges of class. Middle-class feminists, it is argued, have stereotyped working-class women – portraying them in cartoons as the Mrs Mops of this world, reproducing the comic assumptions of social passivity.[12] Middle-class values have tended to dominate the movement, silencing the voices of working-class women, 'denying them a language, banning them, from self-expression, labelling them ignorant, stupid, coarse, bombastic, rough, uneducated, ineffectual'.[13] And middle-class concerns have shaped the priorities of the movement, dictating the demands that have dominated campaigns.

Recent debates within the National Abortion Campaign (since resolved by the formation of two separate campaigning bodies, the old NAC and the new Women's Reproductive Rights Campaign) provide a particularly sharp example. From its formation in 1975, the main activity of the abortion campaign was to defend the 1967 Abortion Act against successive Private Members' Bills which sought to restrict further the conditions under which a woman could seek an abortion – and though all those involved regretted this limited focus (the 1967 Act was not itself such a dream) it emerged as the major concern. 'A woman's right to choose' was the dominant campaigning slogan: her right to decide for herself – not at the whim of her GP or gynaecologist – whether she needed an abortion. But against the backdrop of eugenicist suggestions – as in Sir Keith Joseph's infamous speech on the dangers of low-grade babies swamping the population – this should not have been the only issue. Working-class women, and even more so, *black* working class women, could find themselves more threatened by pressures *to* abort than medical resistance to abortion, for where a white, middle class, married woman can experience great difficulty in persuading her doctor to recommend a termination, a woman living on social security in an inner-city slum can face the opposite problem. 'Abortion, fine, but why not have yourself sterilised at the same time?' Or 'Abortion, yes, and we'll inject you with Depo-Provera to prevent any future mistakes.' The more dangerous forms of contraception, such as Depo-Provera or relatively untested IUDs, are typically tried out on Third World women and women in working-class communities, and in America poorer women have found themselves sterilised without their consent in the course of an abortion. To take up the provision of free abortion on demand as if this was the only reproductive issue was to ignore these wider concerns – and that this nonetheless defined the campaign for so long hints at a myopia of middle-class women.

With criticism from within as well as from without, the question of class has become more heated; we can no longer dismiss those who raise it as engaging with class only to deny the oppression of women. The questions must surely be faced. Is the women's movement – either historically or today – bounded by the narrower concerns of middle-class women? Has it, through its priorities and practices, excluded and denied the experiences of working-class women? Does the related preponderance of *white* middle-class women leave the movement exposed to accusations of racism? When we make gender our mobilising concern, do we thereby relegate class and race to secondary importance? And when we talk of the politics of 'women's oppression', can those who face other burning oppressions begin to respond to this call? As already noted, it is through the issue of race and racism that such questions have been most recently posed, and black women are engaged on developing their answers. Given the way that racism operates in Britain, class has been a major sub-text in discussions of race, but with its history inevitably truncated, for it was not until after the Second World War that race became such a significant divide. My concern here is to supplement such work by focussing more directly on divisions by class, turning my attention to both nineteenth and twentieth centuries.

Class I believe matters, but as should become clear in the course of this book, I think the ways in which it has re-entered discussion are limited and potentially disabling. Framed too much in the language of privilege, they lead us to a hierarchy of oppression. The notion of privilege has tended to dominate debate: the privileges of heterosexual women who derive their comfort and support from the men who subordinate and control; the privileges of middle-class women whose money and education cushions their exposure to the female condition; the privileges of white women who can shelter behind the advantages of race. The result is too often a hierarchy of the oppressed (in which white middle-class heterosexual women hardly score as victims at all) and in our catalogue of those who have suffered the most we lose sight of more crucial concerns. It is not who is worst off that should focus our minds: rather how much has our politics recognised difference? How sensitive is feminism to divisions by class?

It is part of the argument of this book that when we make our feminism the answer to all problems, we push it in a dangerous direction; indeed if we want to explain why so few women consciously embrace the label of feminist (it is worth remembering that these are a tiny minority of the middle as well as the working class) we do not have to look far. The label sounds much too simple. It carries with it the implication that this is all that matters, that women's oppression as women is the final word in the tale of all our woes. No matter that most feminists you meet will be quick to point to other issues: to poverty and famine and the threat of nuclear war. The fact remains that in calling ourselves feminists we seem to prioritise the experience and oppression of women, and for the majority of women this oversimplifies their lives.

It is however also part of the argument of this book that few periods of feminism have been guilty of such gross simplicity. There may be strands today that seek to evacuate class and race entirely from the vocabulary: influential writings such as Mary Daly's *Gyn/Ecology* or Dale Spender's mammoth *History of Ideas* do treat women's oppression as an ahistorical abstraction in which the patterns repeat themselves tirelessly over continents and centuries – woman is woman, our story always the same.[14] But whatever criticisms we may want to level at feminism in general, its history has rarely been so single-minded; women have continually tussled with problems of priority, dragging ourselves first in one direction and then another as different oppressions have come to the fore. We have been torn between competing alliances, never quite sure where to look for our friends. And the problem remains today. Should working-class women, for example, throw in their lot with the labour movement when history has shown how thoroughly male its preoccupations can be? Should black women throw in their lot with the black community, when this community so often speaks with the voices of men? Should all identify first and foremost with the women's movement, when this can mean relegating the issues of race and class to secondary importance?

These are not easy questions, and they do not lead to simple answers. And however critical we may be of the choices made by our predecessors, they too were the products of complex dilemmas.

If with hindsight we feel we can identify mistakes, at the time we might easily have joined in their errors. Just for a starter, take one particularly excruciating example from the history of American feminism, as documented in Angela Davis' *Women, Race and Class*.[15] The women's movement developed in nineteenth-century America in the context of a slave society, with many of its foremost activists deeply involved in the abolitionist campaign. Working-class women donated money from their wages while middle-class women gave of both money and time: pioneers of American feminism like the Grimké sisters, Lucretia Mott, and Elizabeth Cady Stanton all took part in the anti-slavery campaigns. But in a pattern that was to be repeated more than a hundred years on, women learnt of their subordination as women while agitating for the rights of those who were black. All through the 1830s they were being excluded from anti-slavery platforms and decisions, told it was inappropriate for women to take a leading role, unwise for them to address audiences that were mixed. In 1840 they were refused entry to the massive World Anti-Slavery Convention and their patience finally gave out. Within a few years they had organised the first feminist convention in America, with a founding document that drew on the Declaration of Independence to assert the equal rights of women with men.

Born as it was out of the abolitionist struggle, American feminism began in a great affirmation of the unity of these two struggles. And as long as the issue was abolition of *slavery*, the alliance remained secure. Inspired by the courage of the Grimké sisters, who as white Southern women had put their lives at risk to promote the cause of their black sisters, and cemented by the commitment of Frederick Douglas who as 'the country's leading Black abolitionist, was also the most prominent male advocate of women's emancipation in his times',[16] the abolitionist cause could temporarily unite white women with black, all women with black men. Despite constant accusations that their feminism was weakening the anti-slavery campaign, the women insisted that their emancipation and black emancipation were two sides of the same coin. Refusing to abandon their claims as women, continuing to identify with the claims of slaves, they steered successfully away from choosing between these struggles.

But the story did not end there. As the campaign for women's right to vote took off, it found itself in very deep water indeed over votes for black men. Once slaves were formally free the issue shifted to their rights to vote, and what position should the women take up then? Equality was one thing, but male supremacy quite another, and while no woman anywhere had the right to a vote, why should parity between white and black *men* be such a burning issue? Suffrage campaigners were thrown into confusion. Should women, as Elizabeth Cady Stanton put it, 'labour to second man's endeavour and exalt his sex above their own'?[17] Surely not, particularly when prominent black leaders were going around saying it was God's will that men should dominate women.[18] But then the alternative was all too often the racist slogans of 'women first and Negro last':[19] some feminists drew on the arguments of racial supremacy to do their battle against the men.

The Fifteenth Amendment to the American Constitution gave black men the right to vote, but by the 1890s and 1900s various states had ratified new constitutions which disenfranchised such voters. The women's suffrage organisations failed to take a stand; worse still, they drew on the fears of a working class, black and immigrant vote to strengthen their own case for the vote. The 1893 conference of the National American Women's Suffrage Associations passed a deeply depressing resolution:

> that without expressing any opinion on the proper qualifications for voting, we call attention to the significant facts that in every State there are more women who can read and write than the whole number of illiterate male voters; more white women who can read and write than all negro voters; more American women who can read and write than all foreign voters; so that the enfranchisement of such women would settle the vexed question of rule by illiteracy, whether of home-grown or foreign-born production.[20]

Class was pulling one way and race another, while the politics of gender was growing murkier still in between.

This was a low point indeed in the history of American feminism, and today we might claim to be more enlightened. But the issue of priority will not go away. Again and again we face situations where the imperatives of gender seem to conflict with those of class or race. We organise a reclaim the night demonstration through an area where women are sexually harassed – but it is an area where many Afro-Caribbean people live, and our activities fuel racist stereotypes of bands of marauding blacks. We challenge an apprenticeship scheme that has excluded girls from training – and we find ourselves linked with employers in an attack on union power. We call on local councils to provide nurseries for their staff – and we are told this unfairly privileges those women with better paid jobs, leaving millions worse off still trapped in their homes. Some of the dilemmas are the familiar ones from a time of recession: we are pressed to choose between needs we know are equally urgent. But others have a sharper edge. Class and race and gender are *not* parallel oppressions, and the route dictated by one may well diverge from the routes dictated by others.

We live in a class society that is also structured by gender, which means that men and women experience class in different ways, and that potential unities of class are disrupted by conflicts of gender. To put the emphasis the other way round: we live in a gender order that is also structured by class, which means that women experience their womanhood in different ways, and that their unity as women is continually disrupted by conflicts of class. Draw in race to complete the triangle and you can see how complex the geometry becomes. No one is 'just' a worker, 'just' a woman, 'just' black. The notion that our politics can simply reflect *one* of our identities seems implausible in the extreme; there is no neat symmetry between the different oppressions, and those who are our allies on one front may well turn out enemies on another. We cannot always have it both ways, and when the conflict arises we are forced to say which matters most. The mere fact that such conflicts may arise is not in itself an indictment: what matters is how we cope with them. That there *is* a tension between the politics of gender, the politics of class, the politics of race, is something we should take for granted, and it would be as naive to expect feminism to be free from such tensions as it would be ungenerous to dismiss it when it fails to solve all problems.

The complexities of this world we inhabit make up part of our dilemma; they are further compounded by the complexities of the feminist project. The nature of women's oppression does not point to a neat and easy solution, and the choices faced through the centuries have rarely been between 'right' and 'wrong' ideas. The forces that keep us in our place operate at so many levels: how do you decide your line of attack? Is it to be sexuality, ideology, work, the family? – whichever you choose may conflict with the others. How, for example, do you formulate demands that will reflect both women's needs as workers *and* women's needs as mothers – how do you campaign on one front without thereby subordinating the tasks on the other? How do you resolve the tensions women have experienced between insisting on their equality with men and insisting on their difference? Do you look to an androgynous future where sexual difference is confounded? or do you assert the superior qualities of women? Do you call for equal treatment regardless of sex? or for protective legislation that acknowledges women's role as child-bearers? Do you battle for wider opportunities of full-time employment? or accept that part-time work will be the choice for many women and focus on improving its status? And ever tactically and recurrently, at what point do you accept what you know is compromise? When do you agree a first stage of reform?

These are agonising cliff-hangers; a plethora of difficult questions with a dearth of easy answers. And if one of the complicating things that has happened in the history of feminism is that the women's movement has tried to simplify in the name of gender, another is that choices have become codified in class terms. Today the demand for free abortion on demand could come to be regarded as a primarily middle-class issue; at the turn of the century it was the campaign for the vote that was said to be a middle-class concern; through both nineteenth and twentieth centuries, campaigns for equal access to paid employment were often derided as reflecting the needs of middle-class women, while campaigns for improving women's condition as mothers were presented as the dominant working-class concern. Because women's experience *is* class as well as gender defined, the priority they give to different campaigns is sure to be coloured by class. Yet the fact remains that women have needed *all* these campaigns – for free abortion, for the right to vote, for the right to better paid jobs, for the right to improved pre- and ante-natal care, for the right to a family allowance – and that all of them have found supporters among middle and working class alike. So in examining and understanding class differences in the experience of women, in looking at how such differences may throw up varying sets of priorities and conflicting courses of action, we have to beware of any simple identification of some issues as 'middle class' and others as 'working class'. Feminism is a complex project, and as we try to integrate class into our perception of gender, it does not help if we employ class to discredit what have been and remain important concerns.

At the end of the day, the real issues about class in the

women's movement relate not to a hierarchy of oppression but to the problems of unity, of alliance across what is difference, of troubled choices between competing demands. Our history has been full of advances and retreats, periods when anger against men dominated the horizon, succeeded by apparent quiescence in the face of what looked like more pressing concerns. We do not solve these recurring dilemmas by simply re-asserting the centrality of gender; but nor do we solve them by abandoning what has been a powerful feminist critique of the dominance of class. We have to think through what class has meant for women – how our experience as women has structured our experience of class, how our contrasting experiences of class have structured our perceptions as women. And in approaching this we have to start (as I do in Chapter 2) with examining what we mean by the notion of class, looking at the contradictory ways in which we tend to employ the term, and the problems feminists have faced in integrating the category of women into its language. In Chapter 3 we can go on to look historically at what 'working class' and 'middle class' have meant for women through the nineteenth and twentieth centuries, tracing the convergences over this period in the female experience – the decline in the number of children women bore, the collapse in domestic service, and the development of paid employment as the typical experience for women of both classes – but noting at the same time the new gap that has opened up between the kind of paid jobs that women now do. In Chapter 4 we can turn to the women's movement as it developed from the late eighteenth through to the mid-twentieth century, focussing here on the moments when tensions of class entered into feminist campaigns. Finally in Chapter 5 we can bring the story up to date, looking at the experience both of the contemporary women's movement and of women organised (whether as self-conscious feminists or not) within the unions and Labour Party. The problems that class has brought in its train have not been static; they have shifted and developed throughout these years. If there is one thing that remains constant it is that there are no simplicities, that women are inevitably tossed between conflicting allegiances, that divided loyalties define our lives.

2 Class Matters

One problem in identifying the differences between women is that we are both so vague and yet so confident over what we mean by class. Just a few moment's acquaintance, and most of us will happily volunteer an opinion on another woman's class, for it is a label we employ all the time to place ourselves and those we meet. Sometimes it is ambiguous, sometimes we have our doubts, but rather than admit to no opinion at all, most of us will then resort to the qualifying adjectives of 'upper' and 'lower': 'upper working class', 'lower middle class', 'upper middle class'. If we cannot place someone immediately as either working or middle class, we try out our finer distinctions.

Class is deeply engraved in our culture, yet what it stands for can be surprisingly hard to define, and when we turn to our own biographies we are often at a loss to say just what we are. For myself as a schoolgirl, I was thoroughly convinced that I must be working class, for my parents were short of money, my uncles worked in manual trades – and what seemed most important of all in my adolescence, I said dinner instead of lunch. In the claustrophic environment of a middle-class girls' school, I felt simultaneously proud and ashamed of the fact, embarrassed by what I feared was my cultural poverty yet inclined to despise what I saw as the privileges of those around me. In my progress through university to the relative securities of an academic job I then found myself occupying an uncomfortable middle ground, quick to assume the trappings of a new lifestyle yet reluctant to abandon my claims as a member of the working class. The credentials became more and more shaky – they were never that strong! – but it was a long time before I could admit that I might be middle class, and indeed in retrospect that I had probably always been so.

From a different background a friend once described her own initiation into these mysteries, which in her case entailed a journey in the opposite direction. A teacher in secondary school had asked each girl to say which class she came from, and in a response which would have gratified 1950s students of social mobility, many replied that they must be middle class for their parents had a colour TV. Only as the teacher went on to talk of the workers as those who produced the wealth of society – introducing for perhaps the first time the notion that being working class was something to be proud of – did the girls come to perceive that their objective status might in fact be working class.

Accounts like these are just the tip of the iceberg and they hint at major discrepancies in our perceptions of class. At one time we operated with what seemed a straightforward distinction between manual and non-manual workers, taking this as the chasm that marked our differential access to income, security and power. The 'never-had-it-so-good' post-war boom jarred this convention, for it brought unprecedented improvements in average living standards and promised new opportunities for social mobility via the free system of public education. Our understanding of class was inevitably disturbed. Average incomes soared; luxury commodities like that colour TV were made widely available through the cheapening techniques of mass production; the income gap between at least the skilled manual workers and those in non-manual jobs began to close, as did the gap in terms of working hours, holidays and pension rights. The 1950s was the age of the 'affluent worker', when a generation of sociologists proclaimed the end of class society, and went out, questionnaires in hand, to investigate the 'embourgeoisement' of the working class. And if their findings rarely confirmed the initial pronouncements, this did not dissolve the problem: the boundary between manual and non-manual workers had undoubtedly shifted, and what class meant was less than sure.

Official statistics, and accompanying them much of academic sociology, have tackled the question in a way that mirrors our commonsense evasions. But instead of those sub-sets of upper and lower working class, upper, lower and even 'middle' middle class, the categories of the Registrar-General have divided us into six distinct social classes, relying on occupational criteria. Depending on whether our work is manual or non-manual, but also whether it is professional, skilled, semi- or unskilled, we are allocated to one of the 'classes' A,B,C1,C2,D and E that figure in reports of surveys and opinion polls. Not so much classes as occupational groups, these get round the ambiguities in our usage of middle and working class, but at the expense of abandoning much of what we mean by these notions.

Traditional marxism veers in the opposite direction, though it too disdains the mystifications of a middle and working divide. In the tradition of Marx and Engels, this distinction is necessarily suspect, for it raises to undue prominence what marxism sees as relatively insubstantial demarcations *between* workers, glossing over the more basic power relations between capital and labour. Class, from the marxist perspective, is about the relations of production; it rests on that decisive gulf between those who own capital and those who do not, between those who employ and those who must work for a living. The kind of job you do is then of secondary significance: you may be a teacher, a cleaner, an engineer or an assembly worker; if you have to work for your living (and it hardly matters whether your employer is the state or a private firm) you belong to the working class. The workers are those who work, a conception embedded even in the non-marxist practices of the British Labour Party, whose famous Clause Four calls on the 'workers by hand or by brain' to secure the full fruits of their industry, and makes no distinction between manual and non-manual workers. These workers are of course divided by history and status and income, and when we talk so obsessively of 'middle' and 'working-class' we are referring to what *can* be major divisions. But when it comes down to the real questions of class power, we are all in much the same boat.[1]

The commonsense distinctions between middle and working class; the more purist marxist emphasis on the relationship between capital and labour; the multiple categories of the Registrar-General: all these have entered in some way into feminist debates on class. The result is that like everyone else, the women's movement has used class to mean different things at different times. Imagine a meeting advertised on the topic of 'women and class': you would be hard put to it to guess what that meeting might cover, and only when you learn the context will you decide whether you want to attend. If it heralds a meeting organised by the Revolutionary Communist Party, you could expect a discussion of the bourgeois deviations of feminist politics, an assertion that it is capitalism and class that determines our lives. If it announces a seminar of the British Sociological Association, you might anticipate a critique of academic conceptions of class, a discussion of how these have reflected the positions of male heads of households, defining women by their marital role. If it refers instead to a meeting of non-academic feminists, it is much more likely to cover tensions between middle-class and working-class activists, to explore the ways in which middle-class concerns have come to dominate the movement's campaigns. And if it refers to a meeting with a Women Against Pit Closures group, it will probably focus attention on the experiences and activities of working-class women, in the context of that paradigm of class action – a miners' strike. All these and others are aspects of 'women and class', and none has the monopoly on definition.

Class as cause of women's oppression

Much of the discussion within the contemporary Women's Liberation Movement has in fact hinged around the marxist conception of class, for it has focussed on the prime *causes* of women's oppression, trying to tease out the relative weight of gender and of class. 'Class' in this context has operated as shorthand for the forces of capital: is it capitalism or is it patriarchy that marks down our lives? capital or men that make up our problem? Take just one element in women's experience – the marked sexual segregation of the workforce which keeps women concentrated in lower paid, less skilled jobs. Sexual segregation at work has increased rather than diminished in the course of this century,[2] and it clearly accounts for much of women workers' low status and low pay. But what accounts in turn for sexual segregation? Do we put it down to capitalism or to patriarchy? to the divisive structures of capitalist production? or the exclusionary activities of unionised men? or to a combination of the two?

Pursuing the first line of argument, you might point to the way that capitalism's search for profits creates (at a minimum) two kinds of workers: those with skills and training who will be paid a higher rate in order to keep them with the firm; those who are so easily replaced that their wages can be criminally low. If the former group of workers are predominantly men, while the latter are mainly women, capitalism can keep the two groups apart, thereby blocking any potential 'wage drift' from the higher earners to the lower. The advantages of the former will not then spill over to the latter: to put it more starkly, a strategy of divide and rule can secure capital's future.[3] Or you might point out that it is part of the nature of capitalism that it goes through cycles of boom and collapse, and argue that to smooth out its path it draws on women as a 'reserve army of labour' – workers who can be taken into employment at times of expansion, but shunted back into the privacy of their homes at times of recession.[4] You might note further that capitalism has organised work as an activity separate from the home, for instead of the household being the place where production occurs – as it was for example, for the self-employed weavers and spinners before the industrial revolution – wage-earners for capital go *out* to their job. Men have become the breadwinners, women the home-bound dependants, and when they nonetheless do take up jobs they are paid by pin-money's pitiful standards.[5] And while such arguments have been pursued from a variety of theoretical persuasions, what binds them together is that all in principle search out a root cause in the nature of capitalist production. In this sense they identify 'class' as the major determinant of the oppression in women's lives.

One of the criticisms of such approaches from within the women's movement has been that they do not adequately explain why *women* end up at the bottom of the scale, for if all that matters is that there have to be two types of workers, or that some group or other must act as a reserve army of labour, why is it women who fall into these traps? After all, capitalism *has* sought female employment, not just in the lower reaches of unskilled or part-time or casualised work, but in the areas that men had considered their own. The history of class struggle has been punctuated by attempts to replace expensive men by cheaper women, for if the labour is forthcoming, employers do not concern themselves about who looks after the baby. The crucial occasions may have been changes in skill: as new technology has altered the basis of previous production, employers have tried to introduce semi-skilled women into what were once skilled men's jobs. For feminists the key point is this: in virtually every trade to which this process has applied, male workers have fought to keep out the women – journeymen tailors in the 1820s and '30s; skilled engineers in the First World War; compositors; transport workers; post office clerks.[6] 'The men are as bad as their masters', a woman worker complained to an Owenite paper in the 1830s,[7] and generations of women have repeated her cry. Each change in the labour process gave employers their chance, and wielding women as their weapon they leapt to the fray. The men fought back with all at their disposal: excluded women from their unions; campaigned against the use of (usually female) homeworkers; made sure that women when employed were kept in different grades. There were worthy exceptions, like the London dockers in the 1880s and '90s who gave considerable support to the struggles of women workers,[8] or the National Union of Clerks who in the early 1890s saw that equal pay for equal work could solve the problem at a stroke.[9] But on the whole it was a shoddy affair in which few people shone. Employers took on women, not because they favoured equal opportunity but because women were cheap; trade unionists fought gamely against the intrusions of their masters, and in the process secured their privileges as men.

In her influential article on 'The Unhappy Marriage of Marxism and Feminism', Heidi Hartmann argued that marxism as a theory and capitalism as a social force are both sex-blind.[10] Capitalism takes no interest in the sex of the people it employs – it does not concern itself with who goes down the mine or who looks after the babies – for what it cares about is how to make most profits. Marxism, in similar vein, can explain why capitalism creates certain 'places' – more skilled, less skilled, high paid, low paid – but it cannot explain the pattern which has so universally condemned women to the worst of these roles. To account for women's position in a sexually segregated workforce we must then call on the alternative theory of patriarchy: those processes through which men have established control over the labour of women, developing and securing a vested interest in female subordination. It is men who benefit from the domestic service women provide in the home, not capital; it is men who reap the reward of keeping women out of higher paid jobs. If capital then joins in their game, it is largely following their lead.

The notion that capitalism is sex-blind has considerable plausibility – I can well imagine a capitalism which makes no difference between its workers. But it would be one squeezed by labour shortage, forced to extract its workers from every nook and cranny, pressed to eliminate the wastage of women at home. In the wartime emergencies that provide us our best example, nurseries and creches sprang up overnight, and women workers did the jobs assumed to be peculiarly male. Reconstruction after the Second World War made similar demands on labour, but by then there were alternatives: Britain drew on labour reserves in its colonies and ex-colonies; Germany on 'guest-workers' from Turkey and parts of Eastern Europe; France on the small farmers expelled from a declining peasant economy. Women played their part, but in Britain in particular, this was to be as part-time workers; labour shortages were not acute enough to sustain the wartime conditions. And today, when unemployment on world scale is such a massive problem, capitalism is hardly short of labour; why should it bother to rock the male boat?

The arguments have gone backwards and forwards, and most contemporary feminist writing on women and work has converged on the notion that class and gender intertwine: in the spectrum of opinions between 'capital versus men' those who identify with either of the extremes are now in a minority. But still where you place yourself within that continuum has its significance, for the analysis of causes is not academic and implies very different courses of action. In a recent article on 'The British Women's Movement' Angela Weir and Elizabeth Wilson have challenged what they see as the women's movement's retreat from an emphasis on class, arguing among other things that the pauperisation that faces women today stems most directly from capitalist crisis. 'The *key* (my emphasis) issue for women is an expansion of the economy, and the creation of secure full time jobs for women.'[11] Whatever the forces of discrimination (and the authors do not deny its power), the situation of women cannot improve in the context of economic depression: for this moment at least, the over-riding priority is for men and women alike to mobilise around campaigns for an alternative, non-capitalist, economic strategy. Those who in the name of feminism have turned their arguments *against* the labour movement, focussing on its record of denying the women, thus do us a disservice. However divisive male practices have been, it now *capitalism* not the unions that must be targetted for change.

It is not (I am glad to say!) part of my self-imposed task to resolve these disputes, though it should be clear from my analysis that I do not accept any universal priority, that I see the 'key issues' shifting through context and time. As our male-structured capitalism runs through its course it poses different sets of problems to different groups of women, and what is interesting about the whole 'capitalism versus patriarchy' debate is that it connects only tangentially with the question of divisions between women. There is a half link: those who view capitalism as the major source of our problems may see a feminism that downplays this as too 'middle class'. But it is worth noting that the preferred term of criticism will probably be 'bourgeois', for in the marxist categories that inform the arguments the term middle class must be suspect.

There is in other words no neat overlay between those who argue the centrality of the marxist conception of class and those who stress the importance of class divides between women. Both groups are saying that class matters. But in the former it is a shorthand for capital and its powers, while in the latter it refers to a more conventional divide. And since my concern here is with examining what may be differences between women, it is to that more commonsense demarcation that I now want to turn.

The middle class/working class divide

Marxism is undoubtedly right when it alerts us to the slippery ways we employ terms, and the attraction in its own version of class is that it seems to cut through confusion. Ultimately however this fails to satisfy, for that confusion is an inevitable part of our lives. A catch-all 'working class' that embraces all without capital has the great merit of identifying the basis of economic power, but when company executives jostle promiscuously alongside cleaners and cooks, such a definition evades our sense of ourselves. If 'working class' is to retain its relevance to political analysis, it must capture something of the complex, perhaps muddled perceptions through which we define ourselves, for it is these that compel us to action. As a lecturer in a polytechnic I may note my income falling behind those who work in the private sector, may feel my work constrained and determined by those who employ me, my job security threatened by the pressure of cuts, and I may well define myself as a 'worker by hand or brain'. But what conviction would it carry if I called myself 'working class'? However imprecise its boundaries, however much they shift, the distinction between middle and working class remains one of the crucial ones in our political culture – and whether they acknowledge it or not, this is a fact long known to socialists, who move schizophrenically between the formal definition of all without capital as thereby working class, and the daily experience of tensions between activists from the middle and working class.

'Middle' and 'working class' have changed their meanings in the expansion of white collar employment that has been one of the most notable features of post-war class composition, but they have not lost their power. Within the framework of the welfare state the ranks of white collar workers have been rapidly swollen, as public funding of health, education and other social services generated new kinds of jobs. The simultaneous expansion of banking, insurance and financial services has created a similar stratum within the private sector: workers with a lesser status than the well-placed professionals or administrators of pre-war society, but still viewed as superior to those in manual jobs. Many of these new jobs (and all too predictably it was these that became women's) tell a dreary tale of deskilling and routinisation. But others have indeed assumed a different form, provoking an extensive recent literature on the 'new middle class'.[12]

Less securely established than doctors or lawyers – and in the lower reaches of the welfare state like teaching and social work often earning less than skilled manual workers – such people are most clearly demarcated by the importance we now attach to education. This is part of the unpleasantness of today's meaning of class, for while the possession of wealth implied no merit, having qualifications is thought to set you apart. And in a very real sense it does, for qualifications give you access to jobs which have power over others – jobs where you manage, supervise, control – and however routinised your own daily work, it is far more under your own control than the work of those you manage.

Clearly there are differences in the degree of autonomy people have over their work, and differences in the kinds of prospects and expectations they can reasonably enjoy. The boundary perhaps approximates to what John Westergaard has called the gap between the 'job-class' (which he estimates as about 60 per cent of the total working population) and the 'career-class': a distinction as we shall later see that has some pertinence for women.

> The larger group are those whose lives are confined within the resources and horizons of routine *jobs*. This is work which, even if skilled, involves neither autonomy nor authority on the job; allows little discretion or variety; carries with it

no increments in pay and few chances of promotion to better things after the early years; leads often to hardship in old age; and is relatively vulnerable to redundancy in recession. The other group are those whose lives centre on *careers*. This is work – now or within realistic prospect – of a significantly different kind; it promises regular increments in pay to take income well above job wage-levels after the early years; offers visible opportunity, though no certainty of promotion beyond that; carries some authority even at subordinate levels, while allowing discretion and variety in the application of skills or experience; demands (and tends to elicit) more commitment than goes with merely working for a wage; offers security in retirement; and, while not immune from the risk of redundancy, is much less exposed to it than routine work and provides better resources to cope with it should it happen.[13]

Many of today's 'career' jobs are recent creations, and it was the fact that people were recruited to them from virtually every section of society that gave temporary credence to the vision of social mobility, fuelling all those premature announcements that class was dead and gone. Today we are more circumspect, and the idea that we *can* move up, that with free access to education we have genuine opportunities for occupational mobility, is increasingly under question. Recent studies of education confirm what many had suspected: that the children of manual workers have not reaped the benefits of free education; that less than 10 per cent of them go on to full-time education, compared to about half the children of professional households.[14] Wider studies of social mobility now suggest that it was largely an illusion, with an initial burst that could not be sustained.[15] As new categories of work were created they did indeed recruit from all sectors of society, giving a momentary impression of extensive social change. For one deceptive moment access to new jobs and a new life seemed to widen; now it is closing down again.

Against this backdrop the political resonance of class goes beyond the question of who owns capital and whatever unities we can forge in our experience of the inequalities and deprivations of capitalist society, these are still unities between those who feel themselves different. Marxism has not been blind to this; contrary to popular misrepresentation, Marx and Engels were acutely aware of divisions *within* what they defined as the working class, and made a sharp distinction between the objective category of 'class in itself' and the subjective awakening when that class becomes 'for itself'. But the problem I think goes further. The political and social categories through which we live our lives rarely coincide with the economic categories of capital and labour, and the lack of coincidence is more than time lag. For women in particular, class can refer to a whole complex of work and family and cultural norms, and these are hard to get at within the purism of Marx.

Nor, however, can we get at them if we take class as conventionally used within today's sociology, for as feminists have been quick to point out, non-marxist class analysis has been equally resistant to matters of gender. In both popular and sociological usage, it has long been the custom to determine class by the male head of household, a practice that inevitably skates over the status and conditions of women. As Frank Parkin expressed it in a since widely criticised comment, 'the family, not the individual, is the appropriate social unit of the class system'[16] – or to put it more bluntly, it is what your father or husband does that counts. A woman's class has been thought to depend on her husband's occupation, with the result that the conventional boundaries between middle and working class derive almost exclusively from the differences between male jobs. It is this of course that for so long sustained the definition of manual work as working class and non-manual as middle class, for while the equations verge on the ludicrous when applied to female employment, they have a rough consistency as applied to men. The low paid and routinised clerical or sales work that is the typical 'white collar' work for women can hardly be described as middle class; only while we averted our eyes from women's occupations to focus exclusively on men did the simplistic manual/non-manual divide more or less hold water.

Recent sociological debates have challenged the notion of the family as the unit of stratification,[17] arguing that women and men alike should be analysed according to their own occupation. But once you do this some odd results emerge. The majority of male workers are still by a slight margin engaged in manual employment; the majority of women workers are in non-manual jobs. If you stick by the standard definition of class, a vast proportion of the population seems to be involved in 'cross-class' marriages, with large numbers of manual men cohabiting with superior non-manual women. Commonsense will tell us that this is not so, that these women are not in a higher class to their husbands, and as sanity prevails, it is increasingly admitted that a substantial amount of white collar work – essentially that done by women – is not in fact 'middle class'. But then we are left with a problem of a different order. As Michelle Stanworth has noted in her recent debate with John Goldthorpe, 'once women in routine non-manual occupations are re-classified as working-class, then only 9 per cent of stable working class men are married to women whose occupations place them in a "superior" class position'. But follow the argument through to its conclusion: 'if women in routine non-manual jobs are designated as working class, then the extent of discrepancy between the class positions of husbands and wives is far greater than even 'cross-class theorists" have supposed'. Now the vast majority of women married to men in the kind of 'intermediate', less routinised white collar work that is more typical for white collar men, turn out to be proletarian.[18] We cannot have it both ways. If there is no longer a discrepancy between the assembly worker married to the typist, then there *is* a discrepancy between the typist married to an accountant; if there is no discrepancy between the latter, then there is between the former.

Faced with this we are left with three possible options. We can cling to the idea that a woman's occupation is defined by her husband, in which case we solve the problem at a stroke; we can say that men and women *are* in substantially different class positions, even under the unifying cloak of marriage; or we can abandon the whole thing as mystification and revert to the marxist conception of class. For those who cling by the first, the argument is that women's chances in life are still determined more by their husband's than their own occupations: that their mortality rates, for example, vary more sharply according to the jobs their husbands do than according to their own; that their employment profiles – whether they give up work soon after marriage or return to work soon after the birth of a child – are conditioned more by their husbands' occupations than their own; that their relationship to class politics will reflect more their husbands' position in the labour market than their own.[19]

Those who defend the second option stress in particular the evidence that a woman's economic security (and lack of it) reflects most of all her own occupation, and that her relationship to class politics reflects her own involvement (or lack of it) in trade unionism and class-based political movements.[20] Women who work in a unionised sector are likely to have a different angle on politics from women who do not, and whether their husbands are also active in the union movement seems to be marginally less significant. This is a crucial consideration, for the point of 'class' is not to give people more or less appropriate labels: what matters for political analysis is whether the labels correspond to the way they act in their lives. And for this reason, presumably, they are few who fall back on the third option. It may be theoretically plausible to describe all without capital at their disposal as 'workers', but if this has minimal connection with the way we see ourselves or the way we act, what in the end is the point?

The choice between defining a woman's class through her own or her husband's position is however a difficult one, for if it was a discreditable blindness that kept sociology for so long in its male definitions, there could still be good reasons for maintaining this course. When Anthony Giddens, for example, says that women are 'largely peripheral to the class system',[21] all one's hostility is aroused. But after all, the very power of gender does mean that women may be as much defined through marriage as through their work, and since our perception of class is so much dependent on the nature of our work, this does throw up problems. As will emerge in Chapter Three, one of the crucial features that now defines a woman's life is whether she works part or full time, for while only a minority of full-time women workers are in better-placed jobs, it is nonetheless true that virtually all those occupying the more favoured positions are doing full-time work. Yet what primarily dictates full- or part-time employment is motherhood and marriage. In the study commissioned by the Department of Employment, 78 per cent of childless women worked full time, but only 7 per cent of those with children under five years old; 16 per cent of those with children of primary school age; and 31 per cent of those with children at secondary school. The comparable figures for those working part time were 6 per cent of childless women; 20 per cent of those with children under five years old; 48 per cent of those with children at primary school; and 45 per cent of those with children at secondary school.[22] The bare statistics conceal some major differences: thus the tiny per cent of those with young children who still work full time will span single mothers whose poverty keeps them at work, and professional women whose income stretches to a nanny. But basically the figures speak for themselves. In a society that defines women as mothers and wives, yet provides them with no assistance in the task of caring for children, our work patterns will depend as much on the number and age of our children as on our own or our husband's class.

The problems raised here are not to be solved by theory alone: it is history that will help with the answers. But in going on to look at what class has meant for women through the last two hundred years, we can already anticipate some findings. The practices of class analysis – whether in the marxist or non-marxist school – have relied heavily on a masculine experience, and we can expect the story of class to sound different when told from a female perspective. Because of the centrality of middle and working class to our political identities, we cannot usefully dissolve them into a package of 'workers by hand and brain', but bearing in mind the ambiguities of the division we can expect it to collapse and recompose over time, and can guess that its contemporary confusions will reflect a complex history. Approaching class from the angle of women's experience, we will not expect the manual/non-manual divide to be its only or major source – class when experienced by women is unlikely to be the same as class when experienced by men. And if it is true that the structures of both capitalism *and* male domination have their effects on women, we can look to a story of shifting alliance: times when the unities of gender have brought women together; times when the pressures of class seem to drive them apart.

3 Classing the Women and Gendering the Class

Class has undoubtedly defined the experience of women; the female experience has in turn defined the meaning of class. But the way this has happened has altered through time, and if we look at how class has been perceived by women we can identify some significant shifts and turns. Three voices should alert us to what we can expect: middle-class feminists speaking from the 1850s, the 1930 and today.

The first one speaks with confidence of her distress; she makes no apology for her station; she has neither the money of those above her nor the freedom of those below. The dictates of gentility made her a lady but they prepared her for nothing more, and when marriage failed to materialise she had little to fall back upon. She was trained in the butterfly role of idle lady, denied her chances of paid employment, forced to depend for her future on meeting a suitable man. The victim of circumstances beyond her control, her fate was all too easily dictated by the failure of a father's business, the foolish speculation of a brother, the unexpected death of a husband. At any moment she could be thrown onto an inhospitable job market which had little time for her genteel skills. Few enough trades were open to women in the nineteenth century and of these only two were respectable enough for her – the wretched and desolate existence of the lady's companion or governess.

The middle-class feminist of the mid-nineteenth century felt anything but privileged: if at the poorer end of her class, she was exposed to poverty and degradation; if at the richer end, to passivity and humiliation. Far from apologising for her advantages she could feel herself the most downtrodden of her sex. It was not that she ignored the sufferings of poorer women – if she had the time and money she might devote years of an otherwise empty existence to philanthropic activities in the city slums – but she felt the closure of opportunities to women of her own class an outrageous example of woman's oppression. Working-class women were at least free to earn their bread; the middle-class woman was condemned to nothing.

To today's listener, this early predecessor can sound unbearably self-obsessed, wrapped up in her own concerns, oblivious to the harsher drudgery of the working-class woman, convinced in her ignorance that no one was worse off than she. Eighty years on, the second voice sounds more gently on our ears: it is Virginia Woolf reflecting on her attendance at a conference of the Women's Co-operative Guild. Deeply committed to feminism, she was also a wealthy woman influenced by socialist ideals, perennially disturbed by the implications of class. The conference had been an uncomfortable experience for her, for however hard she tried she felt her sympathy with the co-operative women could only be fictitious: what mattered so much to them was not what mattered to her.

> All these questions – perhaps this was at the bottom of it – which matter so intensely to the people here, questions of sanitation and education and wages, this demand for an extra shilling, for another year at school, for eight hours instead of nine behind a counter or in a mill, leave me, in my own blood and bones, untouched. If every reform they demand was granted this very instant it would not touch one hair of my comfortable capitalistic head. Hence my interest is merely altruistic. It is thin spread and moon coloured. There is no life blood or urgency about it. However hard I clap my hands or stamp my feet there is a hollowness in the sound which betrays me. I am a benevolent spectator. I am irretrievably cut off from the actors. I sit here hypocritically clapping and stamping, an outcast from the flock.[1]

The unease described is something we can still understand today, but despite the familiarity Virginia Woolf was not of our generation. Whatever guilt she felt for her own privileged existence, she still had the confidence to state her complaints. Sitting there listening to the talk of money and baths, she wanted to shout out that these were not everything, that literature and art and science mattered too. She knew it was money that had bought her the luxury of such concerns – she recognised and questioned her privilege – but she was not to be silenced by this. In tones that command respect for their honesty, she wanted to face and explore the great gulf of class difference.

A third speaker, who is our contemporary though by no means our only voice, seems to have travelled a long way on. In a marked reversal of the first perspective she will accept without question that working-class women are the most oppressed; in her guilty relationship to their sufferings, she is hard put to it to assert her own oppression at all. She goes down the list of demands drawn up at successive women's conferences. Women want equal pay and equal opportunities; well, that's so much easier in a middle-class job. Women want free abortion and nurseries: perhaps not such a priority if you have the money to pay. Women want to be legally and financially independent: with the right qualifications and the right sort of job, it's not such a distant dream. Women want an end to discrimination against lesbians: their chances against employers at least may prove more favourable in a professional job. Women want freedom from male violence: it helps a lot if you drive home in a car. The speaker is considerably less privileged than Virginia Woolf – probably not rich at all – and yet unlike her predecessors she has talked herself into silence. All the oppressions she associates with womanhood seem so much alleviated by the privileges of class.

What do these three moments tell us? Not that feminists have grown in self-awareness, from complacency to consciousness to guilt, for though all three characters can be described as 'middle class', they are markedly different in position and status. The real lesson is that what working class and middle class mean has constantly changed, and that what they mean for women has perhaps changed most of all.

Upper, middle and working: the tripartite distinction

The language of class is a novel one – widely spoken only in the last 150 years – yet it has already undergone major transformation. E.P. Thompson has said that class is a relationship, something that happens when the people in one group claim an identity with each other and assert their opposition to those outside.[2] This is undoubtedly true, and one thing it implies is that 'class' alters with whom it relates. In British politics the categories of working and middle class developed initially in an opposition to the *upper* class; only later did they come to be used in opposition to each other. The divisions people have seen as the most pertinent have not been static over the last two centuries.

It was in the nineteenth century that people began to talk of classes – before then it was a world of ranks, of gentlemen, the people, and the mob. By the 1830s and '40s this language of ranks was being superseded by a language of class, though right through to the end of the century people still talked interchangeably of middle *classes* and middle *ranks, working classes* and *lower ranks*. The choice of the plural is itself significant, for even as class entered common usage it was felt as a shifting approximation: each 'class' contained such a multitude of difference that few felt happy with the stark singular of 'working' and 'middle class'. Then as now class boundaries were imprecise; people knew they existed but hesitated to say exactly what they were.

The sharpest divide to begin with was that between aristocracy and the rest. As one social observer put it in the 1850s, the aristocracy were those whose wealth 'springs from inheritance alone', an apparently decisive definition.[3] Even this however had its uncertainties, for there were those with plenty of money who nonetheless chose to work, and those who had inherited nothing but used their hard-earnt wealth to make themselves gentlemen (and ladies) of leisure. There was a blurring at the edges, a gradual merger of the aristocracy with the wealthier middle classes, but still the upper classes seemed more or less distinct: calculated by mid-century observers as one thirteenth of the total population.[4]

The middle class was 'middle' in the snobbish disclaimers of this higher aristocracy, who long resisted the social climbers battering in desperation against their upper-class walls. But the middle class was also 'middle' in its own estimation, for many of its members rejected what they saw as the corrupt immorality of the leisured and rich, and deliberately set themselves apart from their so-called 'betters'.[5] The middle class defined itself as much in opposition to the upper as to the working class – and though today we may feel the finer distinctions of landed gentry versus rising bourgeoisie as deeply insignificant, then they undoubtedly mattered.

For the new working class as well, the aristocracy was often more the focus of antagonism than the less sharply demarcated middle class. When Chartists, for example, described themselves as 'the working classes' in the 1830s, their emphasis was on the *working*, and they were primarily concerned to state their distance from what they saw as the idle rich. As Gareth Stedman Jones has argued, the Chartists were the last of the old radicals, viewing the world as a battleground between the industrious and the idle, and within this basic division there was just a chance that the middle classes might choose the right side.[6] Activists extended a welcoming – if cautious – hand to any clerks or shopkeepers who saw their future with the working classes, even treating the wealthier manufacturers as potential allies, for unlike the gentry, at least they *worked*. This perception of both middle and working as the goodies, with the baddies the idle rich, was also widely shared by early socialists. Much to the embarrassment of their more theoretically precise successors, the Saint-Simonians, Fourierists and Owenites all demonstrated this confusion of categories, talking gaily of the 'industrial class' as embracing both mill-owner and worker, or looking forward to an 'alliance of all classes' which would sweep away the misery of the world. Middle class and working class were not so sharply counterposed, even though 'middle class' then meant not just the professional but the very capitalist himself. Paradoxically as it seems, it was while the category had such extensive scope that workers were most amenable to an alliance between these classes.

Boundaries were therefore insecure, not because you could not tell one class from the other, but because the original distinction was with that upper class. And quite apart from this, both middle and working class embraced such disparate and divided groups. The middle classes included manufacturers and bankers, farmers and traders, doctors and lawyers, curates and clerks. The working classes included shopkeepers and costermongers, artisans and factory hands, teachers and domestic servants. Our own obsessive distinctions between manual and non-manual, blue-collar and white, were meaningless at this stage, and it was small wonder that when people talked of classes they insisted on the plural.

Femininity as a class ideal

Class began and continued as a muddle, but as 'middle' and 'working' came into sharper focus in the course of the century, they did so partly through the roles they allotted their women. Boundaries were redrawn, the typical features of each grouping were more precisely delineated, the identification of class was improved if not perfected. And as the new classes were made, gender roles proved to be crucial.

This was particularly true of the middle class, for as Catherine Hall has put it 'the new bourgeois way of life involved a recodification of ideas about women'.[7] Wives who once participated in the family business now withdrew to domestic seclusion; daughters who once helped in the home now devoted themselves to their feminine accomplishments; women developed what feminists later derided as their parasite role. Their separation was noted, for example, among farmers, for as the enclosure movement speeded up in the second half of the eighteenth century and smaller farmers and cottagers lost their tenuous grip on the land, those more successful increased their property and 'gentrified' their lives. Women were allowed to free themselves from household or farming activities, to abandon the kitchen for the parlour, the dairy for the boarding school. Contemporary observers did not approve: these farmers had notions above their station.

> I see sometimes, for instance, (wrote Arthur Young in his *Annals of Agriculture*) a pianoforte in a farmer's parlour, which I always wish was burnt; a livery servant is sometimes found, and a post-chaise to carry their daughters to assemblies, these ladies are sometimes educated at expensive boarding schools, and the sons at the University, to be made parsons, but all these things imply a departure from that line which separates these different orders of beings; let these things, and all the folly, foppery, expense, and anxiety that belongs to them, remain among gentlemen. A wise farmer will not envy them.[8]

But wise farmers were few and far between, and so too were wise industrialists. Over much the same period successful entrepreneurs were beginning to stake out a new division between work and home, a distinction they made visible by building brand new mansions at a decent distance from the factory or shop. Wives who had previously taken their share in management now lost contact with the business; women who had worked in the household now relied on servants; they were no longer supposed to bother their heads with business, but to decline gracefully into their decorative role.[9]

Some resisted the process, like Mrs Thornton in Elizabeth Gaskell's *North and South*, who took pride in her proximity to the mill and had not become 'so fine as to desire to forget the source of (her) son's wealth and power'. But her daughter was of another generation, trained in all the accomplishments of a lady, including the inevitable pianoforte. Complaining irritably of 'the continual smell of steam, and oily machinery – and the noise is perfectly deafening', she knew her mother was behind the times.[10] As middle-class society developed it laid down new rules of womanly behaviour, and most of them came down to keeping women out of active life. If aristocrats could afford to keep their women in elegance, so too could the bourgeoisie – with the difference that the bourgeois woman would be chaste as well as idle. Women were not to work, either in the business or the home; wealth would be made prominent by female inactivity.

It was gender differentiation writ large, and though the examples above are taken from the upper end of the new middle class, the ideals they represented pervaded all the lower sub-divisions. Whatever the income, whatever the cost, middle-class existence was to be guaranteed by the status of its women, and though respectable artisans also hoped to keep their wives from working, it was in the middle class that female passivity established its sway. The result, as one observer described it in the 1850s, was that in this class women were *uniquely* separated from men.

> In the higher and in the lower ranks (woman) emphatically shares the lot of man: – leading with him in the one a life of affluent leisure, and bearing with him in the other a share of the labour characteristic of their common station. But, in the middle classes, though man in his state approaches more nearly the lot of the labourer, woman would be an aristocrat; must needs spend her time in visiting and receiving visits, or in equally vain makeshifts to kill the time. Like the lady of rank, she is above engaging in industrial pursuits ... Unlike the lady of rank, the lady of the middle classes is left alone all day.[11]

The irony of course is that just as the ideal of the leisured lady was spreading, so the women from the *working class* were being called out of their homes into the fields, mines and factories, and away from their homes into domestic service for the rich. In agriculture, the gentrification of the farmer's wife had coincided precisely with the increased employment of women as day labourers. Larger farmers consolidated their wealth and smaller farmers lost their independence; men, women and children alike were reduced to the status of agricultural labourers, with women and children doing much of the heavier forms of seasonal work.[12] In textiles too, the leisured elegance of the mill-owner's wife coexisted with increased employment of women as mill-hands, a phenomenon that developed so rapidly that contemporaries feared men might lose their jobs for ever. And in a more direct causal connection, as the number of middle-class households increased so too did the demand for domestic servants, which soon reached such a level that domestic service became the largest single employer of women. The angel in the middle-class house demanded a servant from the working-class one – and she typically took a young girl from the country who then had to 'live-in' with her employers. The demand for dressmakers and milliners also increased, again in rhythm with the growth of the middle classes. Feminine inactivity was of necessity a class ideal.

Women in fact worked in large numbers, as the 1851 census revealed: out of an adult population of six million women, more than half worked for their living; of these, two out of three were supporting themselves – and sometimes children – on their own. But as the categories of occupations indicate, these women were overwhelmingly working class. There were hardly any 'middle class' jobs for women, and 'the phrase "working ladies" was in fact a contradiction in terms'.[13] Women went out to work as domestic servants, as dressmakers and milliners, as factory workers in the textile trades, as agricultural labourers. In less well documented numbers, they stayed in to work as laundresses, needlewomen, landladies, shopkeepers. And while the majority of those who went *out* to work were single, a substantial minority were married with children – anathema indeed to the new ideal.

The irony was not lost on all Victorians, and the nineteenth century was punctuated by periodic outbursts on the iniquities of female employment: the 'scandal' of women in the cotton mills in the 1840s; of women roaming the country in agricultural gangs in the 1860s; of women at the pit-brow in the 1880s. Scandal is the appropriate word, for the employment particularly of *married* women was considered shocking, and the conditions under which they worked a degradation to their feminine nature. The incidence of married women working was in fact much exaggerated by those who pressed for factory legislation,[14] and the long hours of factory employment made it ill-suited to a woman with a young child. Yet throughout the nineteenth century a *quarter* of the women employed in Lancashire cotton mills were married, and the figure rose to 30 per cent in times of heavy labour recruitment.[15] Infant mortality in Lancashire was appallingly high, with as many as one in five children dying before their first birthday, and *half* before the age of five.[16]

Poverty was always just around the corner for working-class households, and historians have estimated that barely one in seven was permanently free of its shadow.[17] Only the wives of skilled artisans could live exclusively on their husbands' earnings, while others had to supplement the household income in some way or another. A small minority relied on factory jobs – which offered better wages than most for women – and in the mills of Lancashire and Yorkshire, the potteries of Staffordshire, the jute factories of Dundee, married women were a substantial part of the labour force. Some abandoned the job when they had a child, but the more the children the greater the need for money, and fear of losing their job forced many women back to work within two weeks of childbirth. Children were then cared for by grandmothers, young girls, lodgers or neighbours – if the worst came to the worst by the often disreputable paid child-minders.[18]

All this was shocking to Victorian sensibilities, as were the women toiling in the fields with their skirts tucked up above the knees,[19] the women at the pit-brow dragging heavy wagons of coal,[20] or the women in the chain-making foundry wielding their heavy hammers. Less disturbing were those whose health was ruined in more typically feminine ways: the seamstresses and the washerwomen and the many, many domestic servants – though the plight of the seamstress (usually depicted as sad but refined) did arouse considerable sympathy.[21] But least disturbing of all were those who managed to keep their work to the privacy of their own home – taking in washing, needlework, lodgers, running a small shop, all the everyday activities of a nineteenth-century married woman from the working class.[22] In contemporary convention, married women were not supposed to go *out* to work, but the ban on all forms of remunerative employment applied only to the ladies of the upper and middle class. And whatever objections were raised to the employment of *married* women, no one suggested that *single* working-class women should be maintained in idle luxury. Of course they should work, and if they got a place as a domestic servant (an ill-paid drudge), this would be excellent training for their future as wives.

Femininity was being reconstructed as a class ideal which served to distinguish one level from another, for even if working-class women were encouraged to imitate middle-class feminine norms, the cards were stacked against them. In these years, perhaps more than ever before or since, you could identify a class by the role it allotted its women: gender was not so much a separate structure as something incorporated into the meanings of class. The result for women was that their lot in life was dictated not by gender *or* class but by a complex combination of the two – a double causation which simultaneously inspired and troubled the emergent feminist movement.

For much of the eighteenth century there had been greater homogeneity in women's existence, for as long as the household was the dominant unit, gender relations were consistent through all levels of society. Patriarchs ruled while wives and daughters earned their keep: a pattern which applied to the comfortable and impoverished alike. A farm might be rich or poor, but whichever it was the women would have their job: if rich they would have their dairy; if poor their work in the field. Outside the aristocracy, women were expected to pull their weight. A shopkeeper's wife would serve in the shop; a weaver's wife would do the spinning; a merchant's wife would keep the books. Different stations certainly meant greater or less security, and I am not suggesting that all women felt themselves the same. But running through the contrasts was a single common thread: because they were *women*, they shared a similar experience.

By the nineteenth century this pattern was broken and the contrast is confirmed by the two images that spring most readily to mind when we think of this period: the Victorian lady and the woman factory hand. The first: accomplished but ill-educated, refined but to no purpose, debilitated, excluded, confined, repressed. The second: over-worked and under-paid, freed by the factory from the tyrannies of husband and father, but doomed by that factory to neglect her children and destroy her health. On the one hand the woman with nothing to do, on the other the woman with much too much. The images are stereotypes, and most nineteenth-century women were neither factory workers nor idle ladies. But the contrast is nonetheless revealing. From the late eighteenth century onwards, women were being re-defined on a class basis: for some the over-riding oppression was to be too little work; for others much too much.

Of course marriage and motherhood remained the common lot of women, for while middle-class women in particular suffered from the 'surplus' of women over men, the majority from all classes got married and bore children. And as far as the debilitating years spent in pregnancy were concerned, the suffering in childbirth, the tragedies of infant mortality, there was little to choose between them. Though professional middle-class families began to restrict the numbers of their children from the 1860s onwards, it was not till the twentieth century that contraception made an appreciable difference to birth rates, and conditions of child birth were comparable for all.[23]

But the experience of motherhood and marriage still varied across the classes. Middle-class women might be confined to the domestic sphere, but their job was to manage their households, not to do the work themselves. The daily details of domestic labour and childcare were not yet dignified into respectable life: homemaking as a 'career' entered popular ideology only in the later years of the nineteenth century, with the duties and responsibilities of motherhood coming into their own even later.[24] Servants provided one of the keys to middle-class status – though as we shall see, many households that claimed this status survived on only the most basic kind of domestic help. But however close the margins between the lower end of the middle and the upper end of the working class, the life and expectations could widely diverge. While the poorer working-class mother had a hard battle to provide even the minimum of food and clothing for her children (after the superior claims of the father were met), the poor middle-class mother was caught in a different game: she had to preserve that veneer of respectability which concealed the relative poverty of her household; she could never admit a similarity with women lower down the scale.

In her marital relations the middle-class wife was supposed to be passive and pure, submitting to her husband's sexuality with no expectation of pleasure in her own. Working-class women, by contrast, were thought to flaunt their sexuality – and as the punitive laws introduced to control venereal disease soon demonstrated, they were often treated as if all were potentially prostitutes.[25] These stereotypes of class sexuality are undoubtedly misleading, but as

Judith Walkowitz has indicated, prostitution was indeed a frequent resort for working-class women, with considerable numbers reliant on its earnings for at least part of their lives.[26] For women, the gulf in class experience seemed almost unbridgeable. From the middle-class perspective, the working-class woman was the sexual threat that disturbed the family home, or else the alien victim of her own husband's brutality and drunkenness. From the working-class perspective, the middle-class woman was both employer and intruder, poking her philanthropic nose into other people's business. As we shall see in Chapter 4, nineteenth-century feminism nonetheless achieved its moments of contact across this divide: that it did so in such circumstances is an extraordinary testament to its power.

The strains of the female role

Because gender roles had assumed such a decisively class character, women experienced their oppression differently according to their class, and inevitably it was in the middle and upper classes that the strains of femininity became most acute. For the upper-class woman cushioned by wealth the female ideal could still mean an unbearably empty life. No one should underestimate the intensity of her oppression nor seek to annihilate it with evidence that other women faced more materially biting conditions. In 'Cassandra' the very comfortably off Florence Nightingale cried out against what she nonetheless saw as the poverty of her existence:

> Women are never supposed to have any occupation of sufficient importance *not* to be interrupted, except "suckling their fools"; and women themselves have accepted this, have written books to support it, and have trained themselves so as to consider whatever they do as *not* of such value to the world of others, but that they can throw it up at the first "claim of social life". They have accustomed themselves to consider intellectual occupation as a merely selfish amusement, which it is their "duty" to give up for every trifler more selfish than themselves...[27]
>
> To have no food for our heads, no food for our hearts, no food for our activity, is that nothing? If we have no food for the body, how do we cry out, how all the world hears of it,

how all the newspapers talk of it, with a paragraph headed in great capital letters, DEATH FROM STARVATION! But suppose one were to put a paragraph in the *Times*, Death of Thought from Starvation, or Death of Moral Activity from Starvation, how people would stare, how they would laugh and wonder! One would think we had no heads or hearts, by the total indifference of the public towards them. Our bodies are the only things of any consequence.[28]

A lady, in the classic phrase, was not supposed to do but to be.

For the middle-class woman in less secure surroundings there was the double oppression of this empty existence and an unsure future, for even in the higher professional groups aspirations could far exceed resources. Edward Carpenter has described the financial tensions in his own family in the 1860s, where his father had six grown-up daughters to maintain.

It is curious – but it shows the state of public opinion of that time – to think that my father, who was certainly quite advanced in his ideas, never for a moment contemplated that any of his daughters should learn professional work with a view to their living – and in consequence he more than once drove himself quite ill with worry. Occasionally it happened that, after a restless night of anxiety over some failure among his investments, and dread that he should not be able at his death to leave the girls a competent income, he would come down to breakfast looking a picture of misery. After a time he would break out. 'Ruin impended over the family,' securities were falling, dividends disappearing; there was only one conclusion – 'the girls would have to go out as governesses.' Then silence and gloom would descend on the household. It was true; that was the only resource. There was only one profession possible for a middle-class woman – to be a governess – and that was to become a pariah.[29]

If this were true in Carpenter's family, how much more so in the *lower* middle-class household that was becoming typical in the second half of the century. As the middle class consolidated itself in size and power, it spawned a huge lower middle-class division – and here the pressures on women were even more acute. Middle class was coming to mean not so much those with businesses and property as those with 'white-collar' salaried jobs – commercial clerks, schoolteachers, managers, commercial travellers, sales assistants:

> that vaguely outlined lower middle section of society which, in the matter of physical comfort, approximates to the caste above it, and in its lack of the delicate requirements of life has something in common with the caste below it ... the families of the imperfectly educated but fairly well-paid manager or clerk, of the tradesman who has 'got on' pecuniarily but hardly 'gone up' socially.[30]

These were soon the majority in the Victorian middle classes, and while their fantasies of female dependence were much the same as those above them, their resources were far from equal to the task.

Drawing on contemporary analyses of middle-class income, Patricia Branca has demonstrated the marginality of much of this group:

Middle-class income distribution (number of families)

	1803	1867
Over £300 a year	64,840	150,000
£100-£300	197,300	637,875
Under £100	32,000	757,250
Total	294,140	1,540,125 [31]

Whatever their wishes, most middle-class families were clearly in no position to maintain idle wives or multiple servants, nor to support for long an unmarried daughter. As far as domestic help was concerned, an inexperienced general servant was as much as most could hope for, and a survey in 1891 suggests that three-quarters of white collar households in London could not even boast of that.[32] Yet the idea that wives or daughters might go out to work still remained anathema – if you slipped up on this one you might lose your precarious hold on middle-class status.

For most middle-class women this just about worked out: 'Most middle class women spent their entire lives first in their mother's home till age 25, and then in their own home until their death.'[33] But for those who failed to find a husband, destitution was a real possibility. As our 1850s feminist complained, too few of these women were trained to earn their living, and their lack of skills, along with their unfortunate pretensions to gentility, ensured for many that doors remained closed. The apocryphal lower middle-class sisters described in George Gissing's *The Odd Women* mirrored the worst fears of the poor but respectable woman: the pretensions to gentility in the midst of poverty; the desperate hopes of marriage as escape; the feeble attempts to make a living as governess or lady's companion; the decline – for one at least – into a life of secret drinking.[34] Respect and disgrace, honour and dishonour – these polar opposites meant much more to people a hundred years ago. And which side the family came down on so often depended on the activities of the women. Class status was inextricably bound up with gender.

Work fit for ladies

By the middle of the nineteenth century the basic divide between working-class women who worked and middle-class women who did not was firmly established, and it was a source of suffering on virtually every side. A league table of oppression is beside the point: how do you compare the country girl forced by rural poverty out of her village to live-in as a servant, the seamstress ruining her health with excessive labour in one season and then starving through lack of work in another, the better paid cotton hand who has to abandon her children to the care of possibly unscrupulous child-minders, the governess who has enough to eat as long as she works but will be turned out at forty with nowhere to go? In the patterns traced out by class and gender all too many women were in a mess, and those at the poorer end of the middle class were undoubtedly in a fix.

The problems of these latter were at one level infuriating, for it could be as much their gentility as their lack of skills that kept them unemployed. When you read the stories you sometimes feel like shaking them: couldn't they throw off their pride for once and turn their hands to useful labour? The irritation is unfair – how could they throw off at will what they had been trained to see as their only accomplishment? – but it is a sentiment that creeps into many feminist accounts. Those activists who set themselves the task of finding suitable work for ladies were often enraged by the exaggerated demands of genteel life. Take for example, the 'Ladies of Langham Place' (an early feminist grouping) who set up a Society for Promoting the Employment of Women, only to find themselves constrained and bedevilled by their clients' perceptions of class.

By the time this Society was formed, even the well-worn route of governess was being closed, for when women's secondary schools were set up in the late 1840s, they offered a decent education to girls from wealthier households and gave them an impossible advantage over the poorer middle class. The typically ill-educated woman from the latter stratum was left out in the cold: as one feminist noted 'the usual opening for impecunious gentlewomen, that of teaching, had been taken up by others with higher qualifications for the work, who are without the impulse of poverty'.[35]

The Society took a relatively daring stance on this dilemma, and at its most adventurous even tried to promote manual work as suitable for ladies. Hoping to carve out a niche between the unacceptable and the unattainable, the Society trained women in a variety of skilled manual trades: compositor, photographer, engraver, hair-dresser, even the business of house decoration. But class conventions were resistant to change, and the women who responded most readily to these new opportunities tended to come from the 'less refined' end of middle-class life. The typical distressed gentlewoman continued to despise manual labour, even if this pushed her to the edge of destitution. She would gladly consider office work – when the Society set up a law-copying office it attracted 810 applicants for a single, rather poorly-paid, post[36] – but at this time a mere handful of women were being employed as clerks and the arithmetic looked impossible. Faced with 'the supreme difficulty of introducing them in great numbers into the fields of competitive employment'[37] an otherwise surprising number of feminists turned to female emigration as the answer to genteel aspirations.[38] At this turning point in the mid-nineteenth century, the problem of female employment still seemed intractable, for gentility marked the boundary between middle-and working-class jobs, and genteel jobs were few and far between.

But simultaneous with these efforts was a shift in the economic basis of class, a transformation that broke the old basis of class differentiation between women, to reassemble it in another form. *Lower* middle-class women began to go out to work, taking their place in a changing job market, with new jobs in teaching, nursing, sales and clerical work. Despite busy hectoring from the feminist camp, 'real ladies' held out a few years more, refusing the publicity of such employment and preferring when need be the private traumas of governess and lady's companion. But outside these bastions of respectability, class barriers cracked and threatened to break. The working woman lost her exclusively proletarian character as daughters of clerk and managers and teachers joined the daughters of shopkeepers and artisans and labourers in the search for work.

The story of the teachers encapsulates many of the changes of the time. At the beginning of the nineteenth century education for rich and poor alike was haphazard, and the children of working people had to scrape what little knowledge they could from the charity Church schools or the low-cost Dame schools which taught basic reading to children under eight. In the course of the century, the state took on a more decisive role. In the 1830s it provided funds to the church organisations to help them build more of their elementary schools which catered for children up to the age of twelve. In the 1840s the state assumed administrative and financial responsibility for teacher training: it set up a pupil-teacher system which apprenticed children at thirteen to work as assistant teachers, leading on at eighteen to the Queen's Scholarship exam which won the successful candidates a subsidised place in a teacher training college. Subsequently the 1870 Education Act laid down the basis for free public education. Local authorities were required to provide elementary schooling for *all* children in their area, and rate-aided Board schools were set up to supplement the existing Church schools. Elementary education became first compulsory and then free, a development that inevitably increased the demand for teachers.

It was women who came forward to fill the gap. The number of women teachers went up from 79,980 in 1861 to 183,298 in 1911, and a job that in the 1850s was almost equally divided between men and women became by the First World War three-quarters female.[39] Expansion had meant feminisation, and simultaneously a process of reclassification. The first elementary teachers were recruited from the working class, with a few stray souls from the higher echelons of society. By 1914 elementary teaching had been up-graded and its recruits were much more likely to be from (lower) middle class backgrounds.

When the principles of the pupil-teacher system were laid out in 1846, it had been taken for granted that the pupil-teachers would be working-class children. Sir James Kay-Shuttleworth, the man responsible, later commented:

> It was therefore clear that this army of assistant and pupil teachers must, in the first instance and in the main, be

attracted from the manual labour class and the classes immediately in contact with it, such as the families of the superintendents of labour and of the humbler tradesmen. Sufficient inducements could not, in the first instance, be offered to other classes to devote their children to this profession.[40]

The apprenticeship system was designed for those already in the schools and it was adapted to the patterns of working-class life where it was normal to send a child of thirteen to work or to an apprenticeship. For the middle-class family it was barely conceivable – and certainly not for the girls.

Middle-class families did not send their children to elementary schools.

The mere mention of these called to mind crowded, noisome classrooms where as many as eighty unkempt and unruly lower-class children, often suffering from hunger and disease, had to be subjected to a dull, mechanical round of work and examined periodically by that alarming person, the government inspector. Besides the unattractiveness of the work, middle-class women were also repelled by the prospect of undergoing the training necessary for them to qualify as secondary-school teachers, training which was long and hard and which would involve their mingling with a 'class with whom they were not accustomed to associate', a class they considered unintellectual and ignorant, parochial in sympathies, and vulgar in speech and manners.[41]

Conditions in the teacher training colleges were, as late as the 1860s and '70s, more akin to an orphanage than today's college of education.

The type of clothes worn by women students was strictly regulated; dresses had to be plain and dark and sometimes, as in charity schools or orphanages, special bonnets and caps had to be worn. At this time there were no sports activities included in the daily routine; instead exercise was provided by strenuous and compulsory domestic duties. Girl students were responsible for most of the cleaning, cooking and washing, and the colleges argued that this was necessary to ensure that future elementary schoolmistresses would be able to look after themselves as well as teach their girl pupils how to keep house.[42]

In her analysis of elementary school training Frances Widdowson has argued that because it systematised the training, the pupil-teacher system actually *reduced* the proportion of teachers from middle-class backgrounds. The new Queen's Scholarship exam was far beyond the capacities of the averagely uneducated middle-class girl who knew at best a bit of everything, but nothing in depth. Strange as it seems to us today, when class advantages have become so tightly bound up with academic achievement, it was the working-class girl who was the better educated, for her middle-class counterpart was condemned by her sex to a mere smattering of knowledge. In 1858 the contrast was firmly underlined. The government had been persuaded to set an experimental exam for middle-class girls who hoped to by-pass the apprenticeship system and gain direct entry to the colleges; large numbers volunteered for the ordeal – their results were appalling.

In an attempt to maintain class pride, it was sometimes suggested that the successful candidates had been crammed and that the requirements of the scholarship exam were 'over-stimulating' to the working-class entrants. Louisa Hubbard toyed with this idea in her pamphlet on *Work For Ladies in Elementary Schools*:

> Considering the class from which these persons have more or less been taken, we cannot help fearing that to enable them to answer these questions effectually, they must have been subjected to a process of cramming, which must have exhausted their power to such an extent as to have left very little scope for that general development of the intelligence which is, after all, the most precious result of study.[43]

But whether crammed or intelligent the fact remains: elementary school teachers were in the 1850s and '60s still predominantly working class.

It was not till the 1870s that the shift in class character became marked: partly because the apprenticeship system was being modified to ease direct entry to colleges; partly because the colleges were changing their style and syllabus and becoming more attractive; partly because of feminist initiatives to promote middle-class access – like the Bishop Otter College for Young

Ladies, which adjusted its syllabus to the poorer educational background of the middle-class girls.[44] The number of students from lower middle-class backgrounds – the daughters of clerks, shopkeepers, commercial travellers, and most importantly, of existing teachers – began to equal the number from working-class backgrounds; these in turn became predominantly the daughters of the upper working class, the skilled artisans.

Teaching was being upgraded and professionalised; conditions in the schools were being improved; class sizes were being reduced. The National Union of Teachers was founded in 1870 and began to negotiate standardised salaries, pension schemes, security of tenure, thereby contributing to the upgrading of the work. Middle-class women were able to venture further and further out into the classroom, where women from the upper working and lower middle class had to mingle.

The real ladies still held aloof. Daughters of professional men might at a pinch consider teaching in the private secondary schools, but they still avoided the more disreputable elementary ones. The training colleges did not really want their students too refined: the superintendent of Durham Training College gently discouraged lady applicants in the 1870s with the warning that 'were anyone accustomed to the refinements of good society to enter as a pupil, her position would probably be both isolated and painful'.[45] And even if colleges had been more welcoming, the ladies had too much of what Louisa Hubbard called the 'fancied pride of caste'. It was partly because of this that she wrote her pamphlet in 1872, hoping to convince middle-class women that the life of a schoolteacher could be both respectable and attractive. In tantalising terms she described the attractions of the work, which left the teacher free after 4.30pm 'for recreation and a few pleasant visits to the parents of her scholars, or to her richer neighbours in the cool summer afternoon, or to such repose and self-improvement in the way of books or music as the winter evenings may bring'.[46] The schoolmistress was no less classy than a governess, she argued – though as Frances Widdowson points out, it was perhaps easier to sell the job when she concentrated on the delights of a *rural* school![47] For the established middle class, teaching the children of working people was still a big step down, and the women from this stratum who *did* work as teachers preferred the more prestigious high school sector, where they could mix with girls from their own milieu. By 1914, working-class dominance had been shattered but the upper middle-class still held back; what had changed was the phenomenal growth in the lower middle classes and the emergence within their ranks of women who both wanted and needed the work.

The teachers' story was repeated elsewhere with a parallel lower middle-class entry into nursing, saleswork and, as an indication of things to come, above all in clerical work. Nursing like teaching was upgraded into a potentially middle-class profession – with an aristocracy of matrons who corresponded to the educational aristocracy of high school mistresses, but below them a massive intake from the lower middle and upper working class. Earlier in the century the nurse was dismissed as an illiterate, a drunkard, and probably promiscuous as well; it is much more astonishing that Florence Nightingale ever thought of becoming one than that her family opposed her. But partly through her path-breaking activities in the Crimea, and perhaps more significantly through the training school she set up for nurses, the job was considerably altered in the public eye. Unlike teaching, it had always been a feminine preserve, so its expansion in the second half of the century provided much needed opportunities for female employment. Though overall numbers were lower than in education, they still increased dramatically, from 24,821 women nurses in 1861 to 77,060 in 1911.[48] As numbers went up so too did status, and though the hours were long and the wages pitiful, the job now attracted recruits from all over the social scale. In 1902 one matron noted that 'nurses are recruited from all classes ... in the hospitals a housemaid may be found sitting next to a baronet's daughter, and all the gradations of rank between these two may be found at the same table'.[49]

Saleswork too was increasing, with department stores and chains of shops set up all over the country, and the lady shop assistant soon became a regular feature of life. To qualify for the work a woman had to be able to read, write and add, and was expected in addition to be reasonably well dressed and mannered. The expansion of elementary schooling meant in fact that most working-class girls could meet the literacy requirements, but the additional aura of respectability made the jobs just about suitable for a middle-class girl – one of the sisters in Gissing's *The Odd Women* found work as a shop assistant. But the respectability of the job was tenuous – depending very much on the kind of shop you worked in – and its hours and pay were considerably worse than in a factory; 'the upper and middle classes considered shop workers to be about on a level with the servant class, while the working classes sneered at their pretensions to respectability, derisively calling them "counter-jumpers" '.[50]

In the 1850s the Society for Promoting the Employment of Women had identified saleswork as one of the possible areas of expansion, and clerical work as another. By the 1890s both predictions were being belatedly fulfilled. In 1861 there were 279 female clerks; by 1911 there were 124,843, with the bulk of the expansion occurring in the 1890s and 1900s. In 1861 there were 87,276 women working in the retail trade; by 1911 this had jumped to 366,268.[51] In both cases there was an overall growth in employment coinciding with an increase in women's share. In the Accounts Department of the Post Office Savings Banks, women took over half the jobs in the course of a single decade.[52] By 1911 they accounted for 18 per cent of all the clerks employed in Britain, and 30 per cent of all shopkeepers and sales assistants.

As has become clear since, it was the identification of clerical work with women's work that was the crucial step, for work in this area continued to grow in leaps and bounds and the job became more and more exclusively female. Thousands upon thousands of women came forward to work as 'typewriters', a phenomenon that helped spawn a whole literature on the 'new woman' – that independent-minded female who had abandoned the boredom of the suburbs for her dingy bed-sit in the middle of town, who studied at a secretarial college and took it for granted that she would earn her own living.[53]

As in teaching and nursing there was the aristocracy of clerical workers: here, the Post Office clerks, who as civil servants were entitled to a 7-8 hour day, sick leave, annual holidays, pension schemes and relative security of tenure. But none of the jobs typically done by women was well-paid, and even in the Post Office in the 1900s women might earn as little as £38 a year as a sorter, or £55 as a clerk.[54] And though civil service jobs were much sought after for their security of employment, there was for women the usual twist; if they got married, they were expected to leave the job. In the period leading up to the First World War there were no enclaves of high paid female employment. Class differentiation between the women who worked was considerably less than differentiation between men.

So as it became more normal for middle-class women to have

jobs, the major boundary of the previous century – between those women who had to work and those who could not – was seriously eroded. The idea that a lady should not work still lingered on in the more hidebound of middle-class households where daughters were discouraged from education and employment alike. But the idea that you could tell a woman's class by whether or not she had a job was on its way out, and the final death blow was delivered in the course of the First World War when going out to work became a woman's patriotic duty. In the nineteenth century, social class had dictated whether or not a woman went out to work; by the early twentieth century the key question was whether she was married and had children. By 1911 nearly three-quarters of single women had some form of paid employment compared with barely one in ten of women who were married. Marital status had apparently supplanted class as the key determinant of a woman's role.

Women as a subordinate class?

So *that* class difference had been eroded and was not yet replaced by the difference that dominates us today, the variations in the kinds of jobs that women do. A mere handful of women had survived the obstacle race through the professions: as late as 1912 there were only 553 women physicians in Britain, and we can get some ideas of the struggles that took them there when we note that of these 518 were self-consciously feminist, supporters of one or other of the suffrage societies.[55] Some women were lecturers in the women's colleges, but these were very much the Cinderellas of the university system, condemned to prunes and custard instead of claret and veal. Women could not yet practise as lawyers, were excluded from accountancy, and kept out of the higher grades of the civil service. In circumstances like these the most ambitious of women could hardly aspire to more than headmistress in a girl's school, and of the 800 or so women that had graduated in the 1890s, many were forced to accept teaching posts at less than £100 a year.[56] Two pounds a week was not a lot of money even in those days, and was certainly less than a woman weaver could claim. There was not much scope for income differentiation between women.

Women carried their subordination with them when they went out to work and in the job market their gender mostly overrode their class. The jobs that became available to *middle*-class women were upgraded 'working class' like teaching and nursing, or down-graded 'middle class' like sales assistant and clerk, both of which had a higher status before women appeared on the scene. The price of employment had been loss of status, and feminisation had been accompanied by a marked de-skilling. Wages and conditions for middle-class women were not significantly different from the typically working-class jobs, and recruits to their work could come from virtually every section of society. There were no enclaves of exclusively middle-class work and no notable sectors of high paid employment.

Once women took jobs, the boundaries between them became obscure. Despite all the nuances of class we habitually associate with Victorian Britain, when contemporaries talked of *women*'s work, they often lumped together a range of what we might consider 'working-class' and 'middle-class' jobs. When a College for Working Women was set up in 1874, for example, Frances Martin described its work as if all the women who used it were of much the same class:

> When the work of the day is over, when the shops are closed and the tired shopwomen are free; when the young milliners and dressmakers have completed their task, and the female bookkeeper, telegraph clerk, and post-office clerks leave their desks; when the gold and diamond polishers, the burnishers and gilders, the machinists and bootmakers quit the noisy workrooms; when the hospital nurse, the lady's maid, the cook and the housemaid have their evenings out, and the weary teacher closes her books for the day, some two hundred of them find their way to the place of assembly, the collection of women in Fitzroy St.[57]

As we have seen, some of these occupations were later to be professionalised, ensuring sharper distinctions between the cook, the lady's maid and the teacher. But even so it was hard to differentiate clearly between the jobs women did, and as an article on Women and Work noted in 1888, 'in these days of diffused education, class runs into class, and it is hard to say where one ends and the other begins, and harder still to define the work which belongs to each'.[58] The comment could apply to male employment too, but it was peculiarly true of women's work. Class stratified men's jobs as it could not stratify women's, for the experiences of single working women were too uniform to permit of much distinction.

This is not to say that class had lost all pertinence for working women, or that as a subordinated sex they dissolved into a united classless whole. There were many jobs that a middle-class woman would not dream of doing – working in a factory, for example, as a general servant, at the pit-brow in the mines. And the lower middle-class stratum which proved the growth area for women's employment was not noted for its democratic ideals. As a marginal group situated uneasily between the established middle class on the one side and the manual workers on the other, the lower middle class tended towards conservatism in its political and social values, plus a feverish insistence that it was miles better than the despised working class.[59] The paradox is that this deeply class-bound stratum was also what produced the 'new woman', whose experience of work necessarily reduced the sharpness of class distinctions. The interplay of gender and class was a complex one, but where middle-class women did work – in the schools, the hospitals, the shops and offices – they could not sever their links with the working class. Denied the chance of upward mobility, such women could tentatively explore their unity as a sex – and that they did so is indicated by the momentary classlessness of some of the early suffragette meetings.

But all this shifting of class and gender relations was deeply contradictory. On the one hand there was an undoubted convergence between women from the working and middle class. Whatever their origins, those who worked for a living were never far apart, for they were most of them condemned to a limited range of jobs at comparable rates of pay, and the contrast with more privileged men seemed the more stark. Yet almost because of these changes, the problems women faced began to look like a simple reflection of their class position, and less a product of their oppression as *women*. In the nineteenth century the advantages of a higher class had been moderated for women by the associated disadvantages of gender. Of course money had always helped, but it had been qualified by the complications of a class-defined femininity – which meant that the richer woman felt more comfortable but also more constrained, freed from one kind of poverty to be exposed to the torments of another. The constraints that femininity imposed on upper- and middle-class women made it hard to place women on a scale of oppression, for those who suffered most on one measure might suffer less acutely on another. It was not easy to pinpoint a woman who was privileged. By the twentieth century things were looking simpler, and as the growing strength of the labour movement highlighted the centralities of the class divide, the convergence in the female experience helped reinforce this perception. The growth in female employment sent the middle-class ideal of femininity into decline, and in the process class lost some of its earlier ambiguity; wealth now emerged as a more unqualified blessing for women. The gap between those who *had* to work and those who need not bother was still immense, and now the privileges of the latter were no longer so blurred.

It was this seeming accumulation of benefits on one side and burdens on the other that generated Virginia Woolf's self-consciousness about wealth. The kind of 'middle class' she belonged to had little in common with the impoverished respectability of our 1850s feminist; as she noted herself when addressing an audience of professional working women, there was little enough to identify her with *any* woman who had to work for a living. Without in any way weakening her case that *all* women were at a disadvantage, she wryly acknowledged her own relative safety: when she received her first payment for a published article, a cheque for 30s. 6d., she simply spent the money on a cat: 'instead of spending that sum upon bread and butter, rent, shoes and stockings, or butcher's bills, I went out and bought a cat – a beautiful cat, a Persian cat, which very soon involved me in bitter disputes with my neighbours'.[60]

The gap between a woman with a private income and one who had to work was sharp enough, but most stark of all was the condition of the poorest women in the working class. The acute poverty of much of the urban population had been one of the 'discoveries' of the late nineteenth century: not that anyone suggested it all began just one hundred years ago, but that the investigation and documentation and extensive social concern date primarily from this period. Charles Booth's investigations in London in the 1890s and Rowntree's searches in York convinced those prepared to listen that a good 30 per cent of the population was living below the poverty line. Subsequent investigations by feminists revealed what such statistics could mean to the working-class woman, and from this point onwards the spotlight on female suffering shifted direction, leaving the distressed gentlewoman in darkness and illuminating instead the poor and overworked mother.

Round About a Pound a Week (1913), *Married Women's Work*

(1915), *Maternity: Letters from Working Women* (1915): these and other publications documented working class women's struggle to survive, and demonstrated the appalling price paid in infant mortality, drudgery and ill-health.[61] For those who had to combine household duties with paid employment, the pressures of overwork were much what they had been at least fifty years ago. In 1863 an observer had described the weekend activities in a Lancashire town: 'the men and single women really make holiday', but 'the married women, who seem the slaves of Lancashire society, are then ... obliged to set to work harder than ever'.[62] Fifty years on, Barbara Hutchins described the married women workers of Yorkshire and 'the extreme exertion involved in the combination of industrial work for nine or ten hours with the duties of nurse, cook, housemaid, and maker of clothes, which begin and conclude the day'.[63] As Clementina Black put it in the same collection of essays, for the married woman who also had paid employment

> life offers neither rest nor hope; she scurries through her household work that she may spend an extra ten minutes at her monotonous toil and receive an extra farthing at the week end; the premature collapse of a child's boots is a disaster that disturbs all her calculations; a day's illness is an indulgence that she dare not afford herself.[64]

Whether the woman worked to supplement the household income or devoted all her energies to the household, husband and children, the poverty she faced was often extreme. 'Round about a pound a week' was the income for an entire family, not just a single worker, and it implied severe deprivation. Bread and potatoes were the main items of food, with meat a luxury reserved for when the man was there; accommodation was often in vermin-ridden basement rooms, with nothing but a kettle for washing; clothing, was 'frankly, a mystery',[65] for the budgets of these families barely allowed for boots to be mended, much less for new clothes to be bought.

Vast income differentials lay behind these conditions, as Maud Pember Reeves revealed in her comparison of what different households might spend on rent:

> A middle-class well-to-do man with income of £2,000 might pay in rent, rates and taxes, £250 – a proportion of his income which is equal to one-eighth.

> A middle-class comfortable man, with income of £500 might pay in rent, rates and taxes, £85 – a proportion of his income which is equal to about one-sixth.
>
> A poor man with 24s. a week, or £62 8s. a year might pay in rent, rates and taxes, 8s. a week, or £20 16s. a year – a proportion of his income which is equal to one-third.[66]

The point of the comparison was to highlight the different proportions paid in rent, but the inequality in incomes was just as telling. And as far as women were concerned it was these variations in household income that made the most difference to life: what mattered was whether a husband had £2,000 a year, £500 a year or merely a pound a week; degrees of freedom and independence depended crudely on how much money there was. Though the women undoubtedly worked longer hours for poorer rewards than the men (the joint of meat that only appeared when the man was home) the direness of their situation seemed primarily determined by class.

It is worth noting here the point so often made in working-class autobiographies or in novels depicting marital relations: that with all their oppressions, working-class women were a power to be reckoned with in their own homes. Husbands and children would normally hand over their wages to the woman of the household, and while her subsequent redistribution tended to favour the men (they got their weekly 'pocket' money for drink or tobacco, while she kept only what was essential for rent and clothing and food), the control of household finances was nonetheless in her hands. In a recent set of interviews with 160 men and women who grew up in working-class families at the turn of the century, Elizabeth Roberts found only one case where the father managed the family income – the exception being one where typical patterns of alcohol consumption were reversed, with the father a thrifty teetotaller and the mother an occasional heavy drinker. Elsewhere it was women who controlled the purse-strings, and took much of the initiative in domestic decisions.

Thus when it came down to questions of where to live or when to move to a bigger house, it was women who often called the tune.

> Was it your mother who wanted to move to Newsham Road or was it your father's choice; do you know?
>
> (Mrs Austin) Oh, I think m'mother's. Oh yes, m'mother. I

don't think he would object, but m'mother had all the push, definitely, hadn't she Tom? You know she took the initiative in that sort of way. Oh, she had to push m'father to get him going you know to get one. He was ... he was a very contented man really, he could be too contented really. You know he hadn't enough push.

Who decided to come here, was it your mother or dad, to this house?

(Mr Pearson) M'mother. M'father wouldn't put his name to anything. He was one of them fellows that said he didn't like anything round his neck.

A debt you mean?

A debt, yes. No, the house was never in m'father's name. When m'mother died she left the house for him to live in as long as he did but when he died it had to be divided among the children.

(Mr Matthew) Our Albert Street house was about 5s. a week, but they put it up to 5s. 6d. Mother took the plunge to move, but Dad was a bit hesitant. I don't know where she got the money from to put down on the Ramsden Street home ... Dad wouldn't take responsibility and Mother took the responsibility and moved ... It was a bigger house.

Was it your mother who decided to move, or your father?

(Mr Shore) Well I should think, knowing the characters of them, Mother would arrange it.

You felt she made all that sort of decision, did she?

That's right, she was the leader. There are in every couple and she was the one.[67]

This kind of leadership is not the same as power. Part of the justification for women controlling the finances was their fear that unless they did the men would just drink the money away – and the reality of such fears undermines any cosy image of matriarchal power. But domestic power relations were complex, and the idea that women were a subordinate class hardly fitted the bill. Not surprisingly then, Elizabeth Roberts found 'little feeling among the majority of women interviewed that they or their mothers had been particularly exploited by men, at least not by working-class men ... In their interviews many women indicated their awareness of the limited horizons and opportunities of their lives, but were just as

likely to associate their menfolk with this lack of choice.'[68]
Conditions were not conducive to a unity by gender instead of by
class.

When the First World War broke out and women were called
from all sections of society to staff the munitions factories and keep
the trams running, patriotic writers tried to portray the period as
one of extraordinary class unity. Their over-written phrases,
however, betray them:

> They have come from the office and the shop, from domestic
> service and the dressmaker's room, from the High Schools
> and the Colleges, and from the quietude of the stately homes
> of the leisured rich ... Even in the early days of the advent of
> women in the munitions shops, I have seen them working
> together, side by side, the daughter of an earl, a shop
> keeper's widow, a graduate from Girton, a domestic servant,
> and a young woman from a lonely farm in Rhodesia, whose
> husband had joined the colours. Social status, so stiff a
> barrier in this country in pre-war days, was forgotten in the
> factory, as in the trenches, and they were all working together
> as the members of a united family.[69]

In reality, as Gail Braybon has argued, only a small minority of
wealthier women responded to the call to work – and perhaps just
as well, considering the tensions that could accumulate inside the
munitions factories. When wealthy women joined it was for
patriotism rather than wages, and though the work was as hard on
them as on anyone else, at least at the end of the shift they could go
home to sleep, while the others might have to get back fast to do
the housework. With mutual incomprehension, the former
condemned the latter for their lack of commitment to the work,
while the latter retaliated with taunts about being too fine for the
job and not knowing how the real world looked.[70] If the workers
related to one another like members of the same family, it was only
with the bickering and jealousies that inhabit most families we
know.

And after the war Britain was soon in depression, sharply
divided on both class and regional lines. The wage cuts and
unemployment rates were not evenly spread: while the giants of
traditional industry were being cut down to size in Scotland, Wales
and the north-east of England, new industries were being fostered
in the Midlands and the south. Coal, ship-building and textiles –

staples of both male and female employment – were all in crisis, with localised unemployment rates as high as 60 per cent and substantial cuts in real wages. Meanwhile workers in the service industries enjoyed real wage *rises*, and inhabitants of the booming Midland and southern cities had little cause for complaint. Investment in building and construction, electrical engineering (soon to become a woman's trade), bicycles, aircraft and cars, meant that if you lived in London, Oxford, Reading, Coventry or even Birmingham you would barely feel the effects of the Depression. Boom and crisis lived in different areas, adding a new – and since sustained – layer to class relations in Britain. Poverty and privilege assumed a regional guise.

The point is not that gender had become irrelevant, that the differences between men and women had dissolved in the face of more powerful differences between region and class. In fact the crisis hit women harshly, and often worse than men. When unemployment rose sharply at the end of 1918, for example, the government first cut women's unemployment pay 'to discourage unemployment', then tried to shunt the ex-factory workers into unwanted, ill-paid jobs as domestic servants. If women refused these jobs their unemployment pay was stopped, and few excuses were allowed: a woman with husband and children could even be cut off for refusing a job as a 'live-in' servant.[71] 'Women,' wrote one journalist in 1921, 'are almost as unpopular today as ex-soldiers' – an ironic reversal on both counts.[72] Their new hopes of employment had been quickly dashed and three years after the war ended the proportion of women in paid employment had shrunk back to less than it was in 1911 – only 30.8 per cent of women of working age. The only job that everyone wanted them to take was work as domestic servants, and in the most depressed areas it was the young girls who had to leave home to work as domestics while their brothers were more tolerated in the inevitable unemployment.[73] But with all this it was the divisions of rich or poor, employed or out of work, north or south, that dominated inter-war existence while gender divisions went temporarily underground.

With hindsight, these inter-war years marked a process of convergence as the life experiences of working- and middle-class women came closer into line, but at the time it was the contrasts that were more starkly in focus. Family size was declining towards the two children norm of later years: in the 1900s 55 per cent of women had three or more (surviving) children and 25 per cent of these had more than five; by the 1940s these figures had shrunk to 30 per cent and 9 per cent respectively.[74] But the decline initially brought class difference to the fore, for it was in middle-class families that contraception was most widely employed. It was professional families that first began to restrict their family size in the 1860s, and the pattern continued with a marked divergence between the classes. How widely the withdrawal method of birth control was used is hard to assess, but certainly as mechanical methods like the sheath became more widely available, costs ensured that they were a middle-class option. In 1910, 9 per cent of middle-class people were employing such methods, against a bare 1 per cent of working-class people; by 1930 the proportions had dramatically risen, but still with a middle-class lead – 40 per cent against 28 per cent.[75] In the inter-war years large families became identified with the working class, an image that lingered on well into the post-war decades. In the 1950s two social investigators reported the reluctance of a working-class informant to go for a walk with his family on a middle-class housing estate because, 'They look at you and say, "Oh look at all those children!"' [76]

Domestic service remained the major employment of working-class women, swallowing 35 per cent of all women workers in 1928, just as it had done in 1911.[77] The pointers to its future rapid decline were already there to see, for working-class women who had worked in munitions factories in the war were resistant to what they saw as the servilities of domestic employment and, as Gail Braybon has documented, it took the combined vilification from the newspapers plus the more direct intervention of the labour exchanges to force them back to such work.[78] While the Depression continued there was little way out (with even a temporary rise in the total number of domestic servants in 1931) but relations between mistress and maid tended to deteriorate, fomenting a sharper sense of class distinction.[79] Middle-class women complained of the growing difficulties of finding 'suitable girls'; working-class women seized every alternative they could. The convergence in their lives was too stealthy to note; the unity of women was not central to their lives.

Women in contemporary Britain

After the Second World War, the similarities in women's lives became clearer, and 'by the early 1950s the extremes of difference between working- and middle-class women's experiences, which had been the result chiefly of poverty on the one hand, and a cloistered existence in a home where at least the heavy chores were performed by domestic servants on the other, had disappeared.'[80] Domestic service plummeted after 1945; the typical number of children stabilised around the famous 2.4 mark; most importantly of all, growing opportunities for female employment meant that the majority of women came to continue work after marriage and even after children.

Most women still give up their jobs till their children reach school age, though a good number of mothers with small children have at least a part-time job, while large numbers of single mothers have no option but to continue full-time employment; by the time the children are five the overwhelming majority of women are back at work. Two-thirds of women over working age either have jobs or are looking for them; 93 per cent of women without children; 81 per cent of women whose children are of secondary school age.[81] When the Second World War came to its end, women did not retreat permanently to the privacy of their homes – despite all those boisterous celebrations of their primary roles as wives and mothers. Many went off to have their children, but by the early 1960s they were ready to start work again. Women had been 30 per cent of the labour force for so long that the proportion was regarded almost as natural fact, but through the 1960s and '70s male employment steadily fell and female employment steadily rose. Now women are up to 45 per cent of the total labour force and since the jobs they do – in services and semi-skilled assembly – are among the few growth areas of the economy, the proportion is set for further increase.

The change in working patterns has cut across class divides. What dictates whether a woman works or not is primarily her marital status and the age of her children; neither class nor income make the same kind of difference. Women married to men in manual jobs may give up their job and have their first child slightly earlier than other women; along with professional women they may resume their jobs slightly earlier than women in routine non-manual employment.[82] But compared with previous periods, such differences are infinitesimal. For much of the nineteenth century a working woman was almost by definition working class; in today's popular mythology a working woman is a 'superwoman' ensconced in a professional career. Neither could be further from contemporary reality. The housewife has all but disappeared, the working mother is now the norm, and as far as overall hours spent in paid employment are concerned, there is little to choose between the life of a middle-class and a working-class woman. Most women have children, most women go to work, most run their households without the help of servants. Compared with previous periods the lives of women are now amazingly homogeneous.

But as these similarities have strengthened, other distinctions have grown. As women are drawn more and more into paid employment, the gap between the kinds of jobs they do has inevitably grown. Not that women's jobs are anything like as sharply differentiated as men's; women are still bunched into a narrow range of occupations, excluded from society's 'top jobs', and whatever job they do, faced with lower pay and poorer prospects than men with a comparable training. With all these qualifications it is nonetheless true that in their working lives women can face markedly different conditions – and it is this that can provoke despair for the 1980s feminist.

The largest single group (about one in three of working women) is now those in routine clerical jobs: the typists, receptionists, VDU operators, secretaries, clerks. They are what our experts have called non-manual, white collar workers – though where a typist would be without her hands and when she favoured the white collar as her ideal office wear is anybody's guess. As in the nineteenth century, there is a spurious gentility about the work, for it is clean, requires literacy, sometimes numeracy, an ability to relate to one's so-called betters (usually male), and doesn't involve wearing an overall or uniform. But clerical work is rarely glamorous to those who do it, for most office workers are caught between the impersonalised routine of the earphones and the VDU – where work has become an assembly line business – or the more personal servicing of a male superior, who expects his tea to be made and his errors erased.

Below these (at least in the conventional hierarchy) are the women in both full- and part-time manual jobs: a tiny 7 per cent of working women who have a skilled manual trade (compared with 38 per cent of working men); a further 25 per cent in semi-skilled manual jobs; and down there at the bottom, the 9 per cent in unskilled manual labour.[83] These are the women who are cleaners and cooks, nursery nurses and machinists, assembly line workers and packers, agricultural labourers and drivers, barmaids and bakers and bookbinders. In the medley of skilled, semi-skilled and unskilled jobs it hardly matters where a woman finds herself, for neither the pay nor conditions are so strikingly different. The recent study by the Department of Employment places a hairdresser as skilled, a machinist as semi-skilled and a cleaner as unskilled,[84] and though this correctly identifies a difference in training, it does not correspond to a significant difference in pay. For a man, by contrast, it would matter a great deal whether his job was skilled or unskilled, for in both status and pay the printer and the porter are many miles apart. For a woman there is less at stake: the pay is not so much better in one job than the other, and when she goes back to work after having her children, she may have to accept a less skilled job anyway.[85] Male manual workers are much more stratified than female ones.

At the other end of the scale are the women in professional and semi-professional jobs: the solicitors and doctors, managers and lecturers and teachers, nurses and physiotherapists and social workers, computer programmers and librarians and local government officials. It is not such an illustrious list, and at the highest echelons women are still poorly represented: barely 1 per cent in the established professions, and still only 19 per cent in all in the teaching and nursing and other non-manual, non-routine jobs.[86] But in most of these occupations (nursing is an obvious exception) women are much more likely to be doing a job that is also done by men, much less likely to be ghettoised into a specifically female sector. The result is not just that pay will be higher (which it will) but that the job will have a career structure, offer training opportunities and promotion prospects, involve some element of authority over others, and provide the workers with a pension scheme and relative security of employment.

Women's jobs are stratified into what can look like two different worlds: at one extreme, the growing army of part-time workers, disproportionately concentrated in 'women-only' jobs in saleswork and cleaning and canteens, earning wages that even hour for hour are appallingly low. At the other extreme, the women who have been through higher education, who have full-time and relatively powerful jobs, earning wages that are regarded as good – if not brilliant – even for a man. And somewhere in the middle, the fragile bridge of office workers.

The gaps are immense, and they are further reinforced by the racial segregation that has emerged as one of the key features of post-war employment and puts women of different ethnic origins in markedly different positions. The phenomenon of part-time employment, for example, is most marked among white women. The 1981 *Labour Force Survey* showed that among women who are 'economically active' (have a job or are looking for one) 62.2 per cent of West Indian women, 61.9 per cent of Asian women, and a much smaller 49 per cent of white women have a full-time job; for part-time jobs the figures were 21.1 per cent of West Indian women, 12.5 per cent of Asian women, and a massive 36.9 per cent of white women.[87] Part-time employment has continued to grow – by 1984 nearly 45 per cent of all women with jobs were in part-time work – and for white women it is the contrast between full- and part-time working that carries much of the burden of class distinction: part-time women workers are more likely to be in manual jobs; more likely to be in a workplace that is exclusively female; virtually guaranteed to earn less hour for hour than full-time workers.[88] For black women it is more a question of the kinds of *full-time* jobs they do. Many Asian women workers, for example, are recruited via family and friends to work for Asian employers in the clothing industry's sweatshops, where they may earn considerably below even the pathetic minimum laid down by the Wages Council, and find themselves acutely vulnerable to the demands of their employers. As a study done by Barbro Hoel of clothing factories in Coventry showed, such women are harshly exposed to the rapid ups and downs of the market: peremptorily laid off in times of slump; expected to work up to fifteen hours overtime (and rarely for overtime rates) in busier periods.[89]

The jobs typically done by black women are not those typically done by white, and significantly fewer occupy the clerical and saleswork that is so much associated with female labour. Thus while only 29 per cent of working women as a whole are in semi-skilled manual jobs, the proportion rises to 47 per cent for West Indian women, 48 per cent for Asians of African origin, and 58 per cent for Indian women.[90] For Asian women the difference is the clothing trade; for West Indian women it is largely explained by their predominance in engineering and allied trades. Apart from this, West Indian women tend to be concentrated in work in the health service, and the two together account for the otherwise startling statistic that West Indian women earn more hour for hour than white women.[91] But they are more at risk from unemployment (partly because it is clerical work that provides women with the most stable living) while being more dependent on full-time earnings (for so many of them have exclusive responsibility for the support of their children); their position is sufficiently distinctive for Annie Phizaclea to describe them as a separate 'class fraction'.[92]

The gulf in the female work experience is a yawning one, and we can see why the unities of class or race can often seem more pertinent than those of gender. Yet because women *are* women, they constantly cross over the boundaries between jobs. As they move in and out of paid employment, they may span a wide variety of different occupations. A surprising number of women married to professional men, for example, end up doing routine clerical and even manual jobs, for their lack of qualifications and their time out as mothers may leave them with few other options.[93] Women who give up their full-time job to have children and later return to part-time work are more than likely to have to take a step down the occupational ladder: when asked in the 1980 Women and Employment survey if the job they went back to after having their first child was 'higher' or 'lower' than the one they left, 45 per cent of the women who went back to a *part*-time job said it was lower, and only 13 per cent could report that it was higher.[94] Downward mobility is one of the facts of life for women, and over the course of a lifetime it can erode once powerful social barriers. Women simply cannot afford the same sense of class as men, for the reality of their lives constantly contradicts it.

What we are left with is one very powerful contrast: to what extent does a woman define herself through her paid work? As Anna Pollert has shown in *Girls, Wives, Factory Lives* and Sallie Westwood has so graphically demonstrated in *All Day Every Day*,[95] young women in dead-end factory jobs will dream of marriage as escape – an illusion that should be daily shattered by the presence of older married women on the factory benches beside them, but that nonetheless retains its appeal. The kindness of the older women cushions the marital delusions of their younger workmates, shrouding their escape route in a conspiracy of silence. The older ones know – who better? – that marriage is not a way out of the factory gates, that the young brides will either stay or eventually return. Far from freeing themselves from the monotony of the factory, they may even come to see their jobs as a relief from the monotony of the home; far from devoting themselves full time to their responsibilities as wives and mothers, they will find these very responsibilities forcing them to earn more money.

Yet the factory consensus still accepts the engagement and wedding as the great moments in a young girl's life. The factory became more interesting when 'romance breathed life and energy into shopfloor culture';[96] the rituals that surround each wedding day imply that this is what life is really about. But the glamour soon wears off as the new brides face the boredom of their chosen home: 'We make the tea and then we sit around looking at each other: we don't talk or nothin'.'[97] It is a cycle that repeats itself over and over again, and though for some few women it serves as a warning that there must be more to life, for most it is taken as the inevitable side of human existence.

For those who have passed through their marital moment, the idea that they work for pin money is treated with the scorn it deserves. 'Pin money, *rubbish*. I work for money and so do all the women.'[98] 'These young ones who think they are going to be at home on their husband's money are dreaming. Life's not like that, it's too costly.'[99]

These women know they must work for their living, but this does not – cannot – translate into identifying themselves with work. From school onwards they may have

> grown up with feminine role models that show love and marriage and a husband and children as more important and immediate goals for a girl. They have little reason to invest in school, with its constant interference with their social preoccupations. School provides no connection between their activities, interests and experiences outside school and the knowledge and qualifications that are offered through education. It upholds a predominantly middle-class image of the world and bases its judgement on this. Instead of aiming for the goals and achievements upheld by school, working-class girls turn their energies towards maintaining relationships, in which success is more real and satisfying. People come first on their list of priorities, and this attitude affects their choices of jobs.[100]

Once ensconsed in their often dead-end jobs, they may cope with what Anna Pollert has called the 'fantasies of exhaustion' – dreams of exotic holidays, of travel to far-away places, realistically enough, not visions of a better career. The trappings of femininity (so often despised by feminists) assume a different significance: as Ruth

Cavendish commented after several months in a semi-skilled factory job:

> If you have a job that lets you sleep enough it's easy to view other women who wear make-up as being conned by the media, and treating themselves as sex objects, but I came to realise that it wasn't nearly as simple as that ... You had neither time nor energy for proper exercise. From the dirty, noisy and exhausting factory exercising to keep fit and not wearing make-up seemed like middle-class fads. If you looked old before your time, came home sweaty and dirty and were lined and pale, the 'natural look' held no attraction for you – it seemed more sensible to cover the lines and 'improve' your colour with make-up.[101]

Fulfilment through work had little resonance; being able to cope was what mattered.

For many women mass unemployment has reduced even this option. In *Wigan Pier Revisited*, Beatrix Campbell has commented on the 1980s' 'baby boom': 'one of the first things you notice in Northern cities hit by unemployment is babies, lots of babies, with very young parents.'[102]

> ... in the eighties, unemployed girls who've never experienced economic independence are doing the only thing they can – having babies, either getting married or not, but often staying with their mam and dad, and quite soon getting a council house. They never consider an abortion, often don't use contraception. They want children. Of course they do. There isn't anything else. Being a mother has a certain status after all, it makes you a grown-up person, something you can't feel, if, like a girl I met in Barnsley, you leave school, which you hated anyway, and did badly at, become unemployed, and there's no job except perhaps a government scheme. She became a painter and decorator on a government scheme for a year. She said she really liked it, but wouldn't have carried on doing it. She didn't know why. Now she's twenty, and has a five-month-old baby.[103]

More frequently noted is the other 'baby boom': women in their thirties, in professional employment, now choosing for the first time to have a child. For such women (this includes me) the impulse to motherhood may be connected with dissatisfaction with their jobs, but it is not an alternative to paid employment. As we come up against the appalling inadequacies of child-care provision, searching round anxiously for a nursery, a child-minder, even a live-in nanny, we are battling to keep on our jobs – to 'have our cake and eat it', as our mothers often say. We agonise over our days away from the child, but the task we face is not survival: it is how to weld together competing demands of motherhood and work. Longer maternity leave, more flexible working hours, a shorter working week, workplace and community nurseries, greater involvement of fathers or partners – these are the demands that approximate to our needs. And while such demands touch on the lives of all women, the priority we attach to them varies by class.

This, it seems, is one of the peculiarities in women's position today, that the convergence in our needs coexists with a divergence in our sense of priorities. The demands associated with contemporary feminism are as pertinent to the mother on the dole, the single mother in full time employment, the housewife in a part time job, as they are to the professional woman struggling to maintain her career. All of us *need* the chance to control our own fertility, the right to work at convenient hours and decent rates of pay, the facilities for caring for our children, a household division of labour that shifts the burden from the shoulders of the long-suffering wife. And surveys like the 1982 MORI poll on 'Family Matters' indicate that these needs are widely acknowledged with some variation expressed between different occupational groups, but nothing too dramatic. Should a woman be paid as much as a man if she is doing the same job? Overwhelmingly, yes, with virtually no variation in class. Should boys and girls receive exactly the same education? Absolutely, yes, with again no class difference between women. Should women with young children stay at home to look after them? Here women are divided, but it is *age* rather than class that makes the difference, with a majority of women in their mid-twenties to mid-thirties saying that women with young children have a right to work, a majority of younger women saying they should stay at home, and a very substantial majority of older women also arguing that mothers of young children should not go out to work. Is a woman's place in the home? Definitely, no, except for older working-class women, who by a majority of 45 per cent over 37 per cent agree that it is. Is abortion on demand morally wrong? Are homosexual relationships morally wrong? On both these the real difference lies between women and men: women are much more cautious about abortion (43 per cent thinking that abortion on demand is morally wrong, against only 31 per cent of men) and much more tolerant on homosexuality (24 per cent thinking homosexual relationships are wrong against 34 per cent of men). But again, a combination of age and class makes a difference: middle-class women in their mid-twenties to mid-thirties are significantly less opposed to abortion; working-class women and all older women are significantly less tolerant of homosexuality.[104] Surveys like these are not the final word in public opinion: all of them are subject to the uncertainties discussed in Chapter Two over how exactly you define a woman's class; all of them are open to the perennial criticisms over how surveys pose their questions. But to the extent that we can judge, we can draw two conclusions. Not all feminist ideas are beyond the pale, and it can be age as much as class that determines a woman's identification.

But ... but ... but ... Politics is about more than people's opinions and, when it comes to how women organise, what matters is how much priority they attach to their condition *as women*, how much unity on gender lines is disrupted by divisions by class? At one level contemporary feminism faces much simpler tasks than before, for the convergence in women's experience means we all confront the same kinds of problems – the differences between us being a matter of degrees. But does this help? I was recently at a weekend school for women trade unionists which spanned a wide range of occupations from cleaners to semi-skilled assembly workers to VDU operators to lecturers and teachers. As we shared our experiences of inequality at work, we constantly noted the unities we found. The grading structure in the factory kept the women workers at the bottom; the career structure in the college kept the men at the top. In virtually every occupation, women seemed to have assumed responsibility for putting demands on health and safety at work; in the daily pursuit of union business these concerns were regularly pushed aside. The union hierarchies were dominated by men; the negotiations were conducted by men; and whether the women's priority was regrading, appointments procedures, training opportunities, maternity leave, whatever, their concerns soon dropped off the agenda. As women trade unionists we felt we all faced the same kinds of problems – but outside the unity of that moment, how powerful were such feelings?

For women in particular, the division between working and

middle class has become less substantial, but our daily experiences of work, of mothering, of entertainment, of life, still keep us apart. It would be nonsense to suggest that gender was the sole determinant of our lives, delusory to expect a 'women's politics' to reign supreme. We have to shuffle our way towards unity, marking en route the forces that divide. In the 1984-85 miners' strike, those involved in Women Against Pit Closures talked of their differences with men, their determination to retain an organisation as women, their conviction that women's place in the home must change. But nobody could have driven a wedge between them and the men they supported; the unities of gender had to take their place alongside the unities of class. Black women have made their criticisms of black men, noting their assumption of leadership in the black communities, their opposition to women taking an equal role. But the place of black people in our society leaves no room for a simple politics of gender; the unity of women must find its place alongside the unities of race. As far as class is concerned, it is crucial to note how much it has changed, how far from obvious is the middle- versus working-class divide. But tracing its course through the last two hundred years we see differences dissolve and then recompose; what class means for women has altered almost beyond recognition; that it still means a lot is beyond our doubt.

4 Unity Threatened by Difference

> There is (a) sense in which we are justified in talking of women as forming one class, whether in 'the highest, the middle, or the humbler ranks of life'; a sense in which women whether seamstresses, factory hands, servants, authoresses, countesses ... do form one common class. There may be every variety of education, of thought, of habit; they may differ from each other by nature or by social custom, as much as a prince differs from a peasant; but so long as there is 'class legislation', so long as the law makes an insurmountable difference between men and women, women must be spoken of as a separate class.[1]

Feminism has always striven towards a common vision, unveiling those shared experiences that cross the conventional class divide. Sometimes the unity has been one of women as mothers; sometimes women as workers; sometimes, as in this comment from the *Englishwoman's Review* in 1876, women as the legal subordinates to men. To conclude from this that women form a separate class is to take the argument further than many would follow, but as long as women are oppressed as women there is undoubtedly a common cause. Whatever pressures draw us apart, we have our shared concerns.

Yet to say this is to say very little, and when we consider the range of female experiences, we might be forgiven a sceptical smile at the proclaimed alliance of seamstress and titled lady. For class is not just a layer of difference over a foundation of unity. Gender has entered into the very construction of class and class into the construction of gender, with the result that even *as women* our experiences can greatly diverge. How sensitive has feminism proved itself to this? And what lessons can we learn from its history?

Interesting as they are in themselves, the class biographies of early feminists are the least revealing part of the tale. It is neither remarkable nor illuminating that the first we hear of feminism is from the upper or middle classes, for only those lucky enough to have education could hope to leave us with their thoughts, and only the more privileged had access to learning. Early feminist writers were almost by definition from a higher stratum in society, though some were still poor enough to have to write for a living. Christine de Pisan, who was attacking misogyny in *The Book of the City of Ladies* in 1405, was the daughter of one court official and the widow of another.[2] Left at the age of twenty-five with three children to support, she became the first woman in Europe to live by her pen. The Duchess of Newcastle, who complained in 1662 that women 'live like Bats or owls, Labour like Beasts, and Dye like worms' was from the highest aristocracy and we can take it that the conditions she described did not stem from her personal experience.[3] Mary Astell was born into the seventeenth-century English gentry and lived her life within a circle of like-minded women intellectuals from the lesser aristocracy – most of her best friends were Ladies! A century on, feminist fortunes were beginning to go downhill. Mary Wollstonecraft came from the impoverished middle classes and had a ramshackle education which barely fitted her for the dreary list of 'respectable' occupations – needlewoman, lady's companion, governess or schoolmistress. But she too was from the middle rather than lower classes, with her feminism potentially constrained by this.

The list could go on, but an accumulation of more or less privileged women does not add up to an argument. Class background does not guarantee class identity, and when a woman speaks for women we should not assume she is pushing for her class. Yet we *are* limited by our context. It can leave us with blindspots, encourage us in false stereotypes, and unwittingly dictate our choice of priorities. Feminists are no more immune to this than anyone else.

Dating the birth of feminism is a notoriously tricky affair, especially when every year teaches us more about our distant past. We give hostages to fortune with each claim we make and the consensus of today is easily shattered by the discoveries of tomorrow. But if we take the argument that feminism was born with the seventeenth-century liberal tradition, we can begin to trace out the problems.

To contemporary ears, those seventeenth-century liberals can sound rather tame: they accepted the right of kings to govern, they argued passionately for the rights and powers of property owners, and they left little space for the needs of the labouring poor. The novelty was that they shifted the whole basis of rights, arguing that it was not birth but activity that entitled some people to power over others. Monarchs might legitimately claim to rule, but only as partners to a social contract which clearly defined their duties and responsibilities. They should no longer claim their rights from membership of some divinely ordained royal family, and if they overstepped the mark they should be called to order. Property owners could claim their power because they or their ancestors had 'mixed their labour' with the soil. This gave them superior rights to political representation, but only because of what they had done and not because of who they were. Social hierarchy was in this vision acceptable and indeed necessary, but it was now seen as man-made (the emphasis was predictably on the man) rather than God-given. Human beings were born free and equal with a common capacity for reason, and they then constructed a hierarchy to suit their needs.

It was an argument that fused egalitarianism with privilege, laying the basis for what we now call equality of opportunity instead of the inherited inequalities of birth and status. Developed and refined through subsequent centuries, the basic outlines of the liberal argument came into sharper focus: we have equal rights to do what we will – but this is not to say that we have the right to be equal. If this was indeed the birthplace of feminism, what mark did it leave on our aspirations?

The language of equality gave women their chance and they did not hesitate to seize it. With weapons sharpened by the men, they entered the fray on their own behalf, claiming their rights as women. 'If all Men are born free' enquired Mary Astell in 1700, 'how is it that all Women are born slaves?' 'If Absolute Sovereignty be not necessary in a State how comes it to be so in a Family?'[4]

Seventeenth-century liberals had no thought of extending their arguments to women, and typically subsumed females under their husbands and fathers. But once question birth as defining people's lives, and potentially you will question gender. Again and again the arguments were turned to female advantage, with recurrent parallels between aristocratic and male domination. In pursuing such parallels, our predecessors were not exclusively concerned with the rights and privileges of women from their own class, and we cannot say they restricted themselves to claiming the political rights now demanded by men, for many projected a wider vision. But if their vision could in principle embrace all women, their pre-occupations were undoubtedly limited by class.

As is frequently noted, Mary Wollstonecraft deliberately addressed her *Vindication of the Rights of Woman* to middle-class women. She was not concerned with the 'great ladies' of the aristocracy whom she wrote off as irretrievably corrupted by the 'false refinement, immorality and vanity' of their class. But nor was she talking to the women of lower ranks who were not at that time part of the reading public. Rather, she said, 'I pay particular attention to those in the middle class, because they appear to be in the most natural state.'[5]

Natural by comparison with their aristocratic 'betters' but increasingly artificial, she argued, in their depraved femininity. The message in the *Vindication* is a harsh one and it pursues woman through all her vanities and weakness.[6] Middle-class women lived not for themselves but only to please men. They turned themselves into ornaments for male approval, occupied themselves with adorning their bodies, degraded themselves into the status of dolls. Forced to live immodestly by their sexual charms, they became creatures of passion rather than reason. Women, she argued in a mounting crescendo of denunciation, had indulged themselves and their vanities till they became almost monsters of cruelty and corruption.

Femininity, with all its implications of weakness, vanity, sensuality, irrationality, emerges as the *bête noire* of the *Vindication*. And it is in this, rather than a pre-occupation with political rights, that Wollstonecraft marks herself out as an heir of the liberal tradition. Drawing inspiration from liberalism's insistence that it is reason that makes us human, she denounced the pattern of gender relations that has deprived women of a rational role. It is a message that today can speak to *all* women, but was then most immediately applicable to the middle class. It was these women who were losing their share in productive labours, their role in the family business, their responsibilities for household management and bringing up the children. And worst of all, Wollstonecraft argued, they were collaborating in their own oppression. Refusing their rightful household and maternal duties, off-loading them on to servant women, they had chosen instead the degraded role of sex object.

Wollstonecraft's prescribed cure is as harsh as her diagnosis of the disease – women must resume their duties and save themselves through work. And here we can identify one of the themes that was to trouble the course of later feminism. Wollstonecraft saw women enfeebled by lack of employment; she called on the idle ladies to resume their dignity through work. This could be employment outside the home if that was what they wanted, but for the vast majority it would be the duties and cares of motherhood. Wollstonecraft was here pursuing a different line from some later feminists; she did not proclaim independence as going *out* to work and she never forgot that the majority of women are mothers. But she did slide over the experience of those poorer women already overburdened by employment. Indeed she almost elevated these into examples of what women could become: 'the good sense I have met with among the poor women who have had few advantages of education and yet have acted heroically, strongly confirmed me in the opinion that trifling employments have rendered woman a trifler.'[7] It was not the overworked poor but the underworked and decadent rich who aroused her ire. The danger she identified was not so much economic as emotional dependence; the future she feared not so much drudgery as idleness.

Here Wollstonecraft stood poised over a slippery slope that was to claim some of her nineteenth-century successors: the hint that middle-class women are the most oppressed *as women*, that those from the working class are *as women* better off. The latter had their dignity and self-respect; the former were sinking into frivolous waste.

It is not indeed the making of necessaries that weakens the mind; but the frippery of dress. For when a woman in the lower ranks of life makes her husband's and children's clothes, she does her duty, this is her part of the family business; but when women work only to dress better than

> they could otherwise afford, it is worse than sheer loss of time.

Her horror of middle-class decadence here outweighed her social radicalism, and the mistress-servant role went unchallenged.

> To render the poor virtuous they must be employed, and women in the middle rank of life, did they not ape the fashions of the nobility, without attaining their ease, might employ them whilst they themselves managed their families, instructed their children, and exercised their own minds.[8]

Middle-class women should save themselves through work, but they need not worry about doing it all.

Mary Wollstonecraft was an undoubted radical – revered or reviled as such throughout her short life. The point is not that she wanted to make middle-class women happier and couldn't care less about the others – she might well have been disturbed by the suggestion that what she wrote was irrelevant to the poor. Neither can we say she took the liberalism of bourgeois man and applied it uncritically to bourgeois woman – her debt to liberalism may be clear in her insistence on rationality, but she was less concerned with political rights than with the project of making woman 'human'. The crucial point is that her feminism was born out of that 'enchilding of women'[9] which attacked middle-class women from the eighteenth century onwards. This was the experience that gave Wollstonecraft her themes, but it was not the experience of all.

Competition not birth

The *Vindication* remained for many years one of the most vital expressions of the feminist dream and is frequently cited as the founding document of the English-speaking tradition. But when the women's movement took off in the 1850s and '60s, it was John Stuart Mill's essay on *The Subjection of Women* which was to become required reading. Published in 1869 (though written a decade earlier and very much reflecting the influence of Harriet Taylor Mill), this drew explicitly on the liberal tradition and laid itself open to the criticism we cannot fairly make of Wollstonecraft – that it raised the issue of legal and political rights to a doubtful centrality. Mill set out to prove:

> That the principle which regulates the existing social relations

between the two sexes – the legal subordination of one sex to the other – is wrong in itself, and now one of the chief hindrances to human improvement; and that it ought to be replaced by a principle of perfect equality, admitting no power or privilege on the one side, nor disability on the other.[10]

From today's perspective, this focus on *legal* subordination does not go far enough – though we should not be too disparaging of it at a time when so many laws overtly discriminated against women. The emphasis was not however incidental. True to the spirit (if not the actual practice) of liberalism, Mill argued that if it is not birth but activity that determines our lives, then this should equally apply to women. If we are to take capitalism at its word, then the principle of modern society is:

> that human beings are no longer born to their place in life, and chained down by an inexorable bond to the place they are born to, but are free to employ their faculties, and such favourable chances as offer, to achieve the lot which may appear to them most desirable...[11]
>
> But if the principle is true, we ought to act as if we believed it, and not to ordain that to be born a girl instead of a boy, any more than to be born black instead of white, or a commoner instead of a nobleman, shall decide the person's position through all life – shall interdict people from all the more elevated social positions, and from all, except a few, respectable occupations.[12]

Put at its sharpest by Harriet Taylor Mill, the argument seemed irrefutable: 'so long as competition is the general law of human nature, it is tyranny to shut out one-half of the competitors.'[13]

Competition not birth should dictate our futures, and this should apply as much to women as it is supposed to do to men. Drawing on already familiar feminist arguments, Mill pointed out that we have no way of knowing what women are or may become – as long as they live out their shackled existence, then of course they will seem the inferiors of men. But once free them from the constraints of the law, release them into free and equal competition, permit them to test themselves in whatever sphere they choose – then we shall see. Maybe the sexes *are* different, and if so this will naturally emerge. But why dictate difference by coercing women into a subordinate role? In the words of Liz Mackie's 1970s cartoon, 'If I get my natural feminine instincts biologically, I'm not having you *telling* me how to be a woman!'

It is a powerful case for consistency, but it is easy to read Mill's essay as a manifesto for middle-class women. These were the ones excluded by *gender*; these were the women denied by virtue of their sex. By focusing on legal subordination, Mill inevitably highlighted the middle-class woman, for though some inequalities spanned all classes (most notably the inequities in the marriage laws), others (the right to vote, education, professional employment) did not. Woman's inequality *as woman* became most visible where men enjoyed their privilege as men, and many of the rights implied in Mill's essay were still restricted to men from the middle classes.

Taking Wollstonecraft and Mill as the condensation of many early feminist ideas, we can see the problems looming up. The one challenged the degradation of femininity while the other asserted women's equal right to compete: themes that combined to strike the strongest chords for middle-class women. Exclusion was the key-note: exclusion from rational activity, exclusion from education, exclusion from gainful employment. None of these was irrelevant to working-class women, but the focus was too narrow to encompass their concerns. In particular the problem of too much work was overshadowed by the problem of too little and, whatever the intentions, the results encouraged the belief that middle-class women were the worst off.

The hierarchy of oppressions

When the women's movement developed from the 1850s onwards, it had its own hierarchy of oppressions, but in contrast to today, it was often the single woman from the middle class who appeared the worst off. By implication, and sometimes more explicitly, working-class women could be counted a more privileged group. Lydia Becker, organiser of the Manchester Suffrage Society from the 1860s to 1880s, fell neatly into this trap when she proclaimed:

> What I most desire is to see men and women of the *middle classes* stand on the same terms of equality as prevail in the working classes – and the highest aristocracy. A *great lady* or a *factory woman* are independent persons – personages – the women of the middle classes are *nobodies*, and if they act for themselves they lose caste![14]

That this version of working-class life was mistaken goes almost without saying: factory women were the elite of women workers – which speaks volumes for the conditions of the greater number in domestic service or the dressmaking trades – and yet even factory women were concentrated in the lower reaches of the textile industry with their right to work recurrently challenged. In neither wages nor conditions were working-class women the equals of men, and their experiences of marital independence left all too much to be desired. But the very real horrors of middle-class life had taken a powerful hold on the feminist imagination and any woman with a job looked lucky by comparison.

The plight of the *single* woman from the middle class was a particular focus of attention, despite (perhaps, given the female predeliction for altruism, because of) the happily married status of many leading nineteenth-century feminists. The census of 1851 had sent shock waves through the community of 'educated women' establishing as it did that as many as two million unmarried, unsupported women were having to fend for themselves. If anything showed up the hollowness of nineteenth-century ideals of femininity it was this: the 'vocation' of wife and mother was inexorably closed to many, yet the only other avenues open were the grossly underpaid ones of teaching, domestic service and needlework. Of these, the governess was highlighted by Bessie Rayner Parkes (one of the founding members of the Association For Promoting the Employment of Women) as 'the plague-spot in the condition of our prosperous and progressive country'[15] for her pitiful wages allowed no scope for saving for old age, while the nature of the job meant that many might be redundant by forty. In her zeal to promote wider opportunities for impoverished middle-class women, Bessie Rayner Parkes played down the employment needs of women who were married; and in a particularly unfortunate moment of class bias, she suggested that working-class wives had no claim on jobs.

> A great singer, an artist, or an author, who keeps servants, may righteously afford the number of hours necessary to fulfil her profession, without any sacrifice to the welfare of her children, and there are innumerable excellent women who have combined these avocations and duties with irreproachable exactitude; but in the working class, where the mother is also nurse and house-servant, where all the cleanliness,

> economy, and comfort of a home depend on her actual and constant superintendence, her absence at any trade is as bad in a money as in a moral point of view.[16]

We should not make too much of this: feminists were soon to be as staunch defenders of the right of working-class women to work as anyone could desire. But the focus on the plight of the unwed women from the middle class was typical of these years – and indeed the first demand of the women's suffrage movement was precisely for votes for single (and of course middle-class) women. In 1866 feminists called for the enfranchisement of householders irrespective of sex. At a time when married women had no claim to property in their own names, the only female householders would be widowed or unwed, and married women would continue to be subsumed under their husbands' votes. Many supported this only as a tactical manoeuvre – that thin end of the wedge approach which so characterised the suffrage movement. But others were more defiant in their defiance, arguing that these single women were the ones in most urgent need. Lydia Becker, who explicitly defended the 'widows and spinsters' franchise', again serves as an example: she reputedly dismissed the married woman's claim to a vote with a 'My dear, a good husband is much better worth having than a vote.'[17] Married women were better off than single: working-class women were more fortunate than their middle-class sisters.

Crossing the class divide

With all this, it would be wrong to say that nineteenth-century feminism ignored working-class women, and misleading to suggest that their marital difficulties were always underplayed. Because feminism *is* about woman, it constantly pushes beyond the barriers of class, struggling towards a sisterhood that spans all social divides. A variety of late nineteenth-century campaigns testify to this. The continued campaigns for a Married Women's Property Act were not, as its name might suggest, exclusively concerned with propertied women. Rather they drew attention to the inequities and brutalities in the working-class household, citing the drunken husband who spends all the family income on alcohol as part of the case for reform.[18] The 1870s campaign against the Contagious Diseases Acts was an extraordinary example of gender solidarity in which the most respectable of middle-class women claimed common cause with working-class prostitutes.[19] The legislation exposed working-class women to continual police surveillance, to forcible examination to check if they had venereal disease, and to involuntary incarceration in a lock hospital if they proved infected. Astonishingly, respectable feminists were able to see this not only as a 'wholesale outrage on our poorer sisters'[20] but as an attack on all womanhood – one that symbolised the male power that ran through all society. The attempts in the 1880s to abolish all vestiges of female employment in the mines again called forth a gender solidarity as leading suffragists joined the campaign to defend the women's right to work.[21] And in the 1890s, when the suffrage movement had sunk temporarily into the doldrums, middle-class feminists helped spark off a whole new wave of militancy when they shifted their attentions to the factory women in the north-east of England.[22]

But in all these moments the tensions of class were bubbling beneath the surface, and they occasionally broke through. For a start, unity was often premised on stereotypes rather than mutual comprehension and where this was the case it got in the way of genuinely joint action. With all its successes, the campaign against the Contagious Diseases Acts is one example of this. Feminists had taken a great plunge into sisterhood: they had identified with the prostitutes while still condemning the immoralities of prostitution. They were helped in this by their image of prostitutes as victims and even more so, as victims of aristocratic vice. They fortified themselves with the vision of the servant girl seduced by her powerful master, cast out into a merciless world, forced by lack of alternatives to earn her living in degradation. If this were true then women could be redeemed – and part of the case against the Acts was that they so firmly stamped a woman as prostitute, closing the door on future redemption. But in fact most prostitutes had their first sexual experience with a man of their own class, and few of them shared the moral outrage expressed in the repeal campaign. They certainly wanted repeal, and often resisted the implementation of the Acts – either with or without the support of the Ladies National Association (LNA). But their perception of the problem did not mesh neatly with that of the LNA and feminists secured only fragile contacts with prostitutes. They did draw working women to their campaign meetings, but had no luck in generating a separate working women's organisation; ironically, their greatest success was in galvanising respectable working men. Working-class women had little general political involvement at this time and we can hardly blame the LNA for failing to break the pattern. But class stereotypes did not help matters.

The campaigns for successive Married Women's Property Acts were similarly bedevilled. On the one hand these highlighted the unities of gender, for they drew on very different class experiences to build a powerful case: the women with inherited wealth whose husbands had absconded with their money; the women working as cooks and laundresses whose husbands could take from the bank their savings of many years.[23] Upper-class women were the only ones safe, for their more substantial inheritance was usually protected by deeds of settlement drawn up on marriage, but it was 'one law for the rich and another for the poor'[24] – all other women were equally vulnerable. The legal inequities of marriage affected middle and working class alike, but here too the campaign was beset by stereotype. As applied to poorer women, the feminist case often rested on the brutalities of the working-class man, represented as rapacious, a drunkard, reluctant to work for himself. As John Stuart Mill put it in a speech to Parliament in 1867, a poor woman's earnings belonged to her husband, who could 'tear it all from her, squander every penny of it in debauchery, leave her to support by her own labour herself and her children and ... unless she is judicially separated from him he can pounce down upon her savings, and leave her penniless.'[25] There were cases enough to fit the description, but still you can sense the class distaste. It is a picture from outside: the woman a victim, the man a brute. It may have described the reality in many households, but it fits too neatly with the dominant ideology to carry full conviction.

Protective legislation

The issue that raised the most acute dilemmas of class and gender was however protective legislation, a difficult area of dispute which had feminism working hard towards a unified perspective, but hampered en route by its class baggage. The development of the factory system from the late eighteenth century onwards had radically worsened working conditions: hours had risen to an all time high in the 1820s and '30s while conditions had sunk to an all time low. The gruesome results began to emerge through the work of Royal Commissions, and social reformers of all persuasions combined to check the decline. But their compassion was restricted to the women and children; they favoured not a general amelioration of conditions for all workers, but a restriction on female and child employment. The 1842 Mines Act, which excluded women and children from underground work in the mines, was followed by the 1844 Factory Act, which set a maximum twelve hour day for women factory workers. Hard on its heels came the 1847 Ten Hours Act, which officially limited hours for women and children, and effectively reduced them for men as well.

When workers first organised in the Ten Hours Movement in the 1830s, they had called for shorter hours for *all* factory labour, making no distinction between the women and the men. But with the election in 1841 of a Tory government that was sympathetic but not yet committed to restrictions in hours, trade unionists developed the divisive strategy of pushing the argument in terms of women. Thus in the wake of the election, a Yorkshire deputation argued for a ten-hour limit for women, maintaining that part of the benefit of this would be that it would reduce female employment and female competition for jobs – a line that found ready approval from Gladstone, who was no supporter of the rights of married women to work.[26] In view of this, it is hardly surprising that the first Factory Acts applied to women and children alone, nor that male trade unionists widely supported them.

Feminists rejected what they saw as a blatant denial of women's rights to work, believing (with some justice!) that the laws operated to protect not the weaker, but the *stronger* sex. They had little reason at this stage to identify with the unions and when they saw debates on the iniquities of female employment, they read 'protection' as just another word for exclusion. Unfortunately some went even further: drawing on the celebration of competition that they found in John Stuart Mill, they invoked the principles of *laissez-faire* against the encumbrances of state control; in the name of women, they threw in their lot with the free market.

This was not true of the Women's Protective and Provident League (later Women's Trade Union League), but when it sent its first delegates to the TUC in 1875 it set itself firmly against protective legislation – and encountered much grumbling against the ignorance of these middle-class women. Trade unionists claimed the Factory Acts as a defence against the worst excesses of industrial capitalism and a first step to better conditions for all. The feminists, they argued, were blinded by their class perspective; they saw that middle-class men had excluded women from the more lucrative professions and assumed that working-class men were up to the same trick; they had no real sensitivity to the harsh conditions of working-class life and no understanding of trade union struggle. The battle was fought in mutual condemnation. As Ray Stachey put it, 'The men's very genuine fears were put aside by the feminists as plain sex selfishness, while the ideals of the women were derided as middle-class ignorance by the men.'[27]

Matters came to a head in the mid-1880s over proposals to ban women completely from the mines and restrict the weight of hammers employed by women in the chain making trades.[28] The 1842 Mines Act had excluded women and children from underground work, leaving a few thousand still engaged on the surface. By the 1880s barely 4,000 continued in employment, and when legislation was put forward in 1886 to regulate conditions and reduce the risks of accident, there was an attempt to include a clause banning all female employment. The pit brow women rallied to defend their jobs – supported in this by their employers, abandoned by most (though not all) male miners, and assisted by many of the leading suffragists, including Millicent Fawcett and Lydia Becker. The *Englishwoman's Review* had long championed the pitwomen's right to work, and it commented in 1887:

> We cannot protest too often or too loudly against the ill-considered benevolence which, instead of seeking to ameliorate the conditions under which labour is performed, aims at depriving competent female workers of their earnings and independence, and by lessening the openings for the employment of women, chokes to overflowing and starves down those which remain untouched.[29]

The debate was and is a difficult one. Discriminatory legislation clearly put women at a disadvantage in finding work: women at the pit brow were threatened with starvation by the proposals for total exclusion from the mines; women in chainmaking could hardly compete with the men if the weight of the hammers they used was to be restricted; women in the printing trades were already severely hampered by the limits on night work for women. But conditions often *were* appalling and if the women's movement was to gain the initiative, it needed some answer to these. We might warm to the chainmaker who in the deputation to the Home secretary in 1886 claimed, 'I ha' had fourteen children, sir, and I never was better in my life',[30] but we should also be horrified by the circumstances that forced her to combine such heavy work with multiple pregnancies. The right to work was not enough, yet through the 1870s and most of the 1880s this became the predominant women's movement line.

Despite occasional reference to ameliorating conditions as a better way forward than exclusion, some feminists fell into defending pit brow work as not so bad after all. Working women, they said, did just as heavy and dangerous work elsewhere – which proved not that their lives were awful, but that women were more capable than popular ideology would allow. The *Englishwoman's Review* was opposed to the 'aggressive philanthropy – the control-you-for-your-own-good system of the present day', and cited this as one of the two major threats to women's employment – the other of course being the unions.[31] Rather than fighting for better conditions, such feminists tended to reserve their energies for the basic right to work. And though we can view this as a tactical decision – how could they hope to press for better jobs unless they had first won the right to jobs at all? – it also suggests the preoccupations they brought from their own lives. The pit brow women served as evidence for what women could do; their very existence challenged all those oppressive assumptions about womanhood which pervaded middle-class life. They were, as the *Englishwomen's Domestic Magazine* put it, 'living hammers to break down all your theories respecting women's feebleness, all your prejudices against women's independence, all your jealous fears that freedom for women may mean what it often does for man – an impunity for sin.'[32]

There are powerful echoes of Lydia Becker in this version of working women as strong and free and independent. Middle-class feminists imposed a stereotype derived from their own needs. Feeble dependence was meant to be their lot and they rallied warmly to the defence of women who seemed above all this. But they could not then acknowledge the other side of pit brow life – the constant exposure to the elements, the accidents and the deaths. So when they acted to defend the rights of working women they brought to their aid their anger for themselves, and it sometimes blinded them to wider issues at stake. This is not to say they were wrong to support the pit brow women, but when they talked romantically of working-class life, pursuing the double stereotypes of the powerful woman and brutalised man, their ignorance gave weight to the suspicions against them, and weakened an otherwise powerful case.

The open battle of feminism versus the unions was a relatively short-lived affair and by the 1890s things were beginning to change. The Women's Trade Union League did an about-turn on protective legislation in the late 1880s, largely in response to the harsh realities of organising working women, but also in tune with the changed climate of liberalism which now made its rapprochement towards the state. Outside the unusually well unionised textiles industries, it was proving extremely difficult to force changes in women's employment, for too many were working in the sweated trades or small (often family) workshops. *Laissez-faire* was increasingly discredited; legislation no longer seemed such a dangerous card to play; and the particular constraints on women's trade unionism made it especially risky to rely on self-organisation alone. So while efforts to foster women's unionisation continued and intensified, the emphasis gradually shifted towards further legislation.[33]

The League dropped its opposition to the Factory Acts and put its efforts instead into securing female representation of the factory inspectorate. At the same time it introduced a more radical prong with the pressure for equal pay; if men were seriously agitated about the use of women to undercut their wages, they had better fight for equal pay for all. The League moved and won an Equal Pay motion at the TUC Congress in 1888, making this for the first time part of official union policy. In subsequent years, the League developed its new demand for a legal minimum wage – and its campaign on this was partially responsible for the Trade Boards set up in the early twentieth century. The League's about-turn was not universally approved and most of the older suffragists still stuck to their guns. But the boundaries of debate were shifting: instead of the earlier 'fine fingered ladies'[34] versus men of toil, more subtle divisions were developing. What influenced your line by the turn of the century was not so much your class as your chosen area of activity. Those feminists most concerned with union and industrial affairs (and this included a growing contingent of middle-class women) were re-examining their strategies; those claimed by other concerns (such as the battle for the vote) tended to stick by the old.

An example of the former was the Women's Industrial Council which was launched in the 1890s, an organisation that drew on the services of 'young women of education and intelligence' who wanted to improve 'the social conditions of working women'.[35] The Council was thoroughly committed to legislation as a means of reform, calling among other things for the regulation and inspection of the conditions of home-workers, and working to promote knowledge of the Factory Acts among women factory workers. It rejected what it saw a false dichotomy between state regulation and trade union organisation and, while noting the danger that protective legislation could serve to exclude women from paid employment, argued for even greater regulation and control. Yet the Women's Industrial Council was middle class in its composition, drawing less on practising trade unionists than on 'social investigators, reformers and administrators, whose activities revolved around meetings, conferences, letter-writing campaigns and organising deputations'.[36] This kind of class composition no longer implied opposition to the Factory Acts, for by the turn of the century the context of debate had changed.

The intricacies of the story reflect the complex relationship between gender and class. When feminists first staked out their opposition to protective legislation, it was the history of middle-class exclusion that was often the formative experience, and while this in no way invalidated their criticisms, it could – and sometimes did – lead them into an unnecessary polarity between the right to work and the right to better conditions. A more sustained involvement with the problems of low pay and dangerous work helped correct the balance, but the change when it came, took place within the constituency of middle-class feminists: not because they were being swept aside by working-class activists, but more because their own perception of the state was under revision. By the twentieth century it was clear that class alone did not dictate positions and women concerned with employment issues differed as much within classes as they might have done between them.

Working-class feminism

The point is confirmed by the new current that was swelling with the revival of working-class feminism, for here too there was no simple chorus of demands. Working-class women had been active as both socialists and feminists within the Owenite movement of the 1830s and '40s,[37] but their voices had been relatively silenced since then. Working-class feminism now re-appeared in the charged atmosphere of the 1890s – in the context of the *Clarion* club, the Independent Labour Party, the Women's Co-operative Guild. The most active were those women in waged employment, and the Lancashire textile unions proved a particularly fertile ground for a new wave of political campaigns which ranged through struggles for equal pay and better conditions, for the right of women to work, to the right of women to vote.[38] And interestingly enough, these women re-affirmed what sounded like the older feminist critique of protective legislation; in 1907-8, for example, they led a lively campaign against a proposal to extend restrictions on women's evening employment which was threatening in particular the right of barmaids to work.[39] The new radical suffragists did not support the line of the Women's Trade Union League, and indeed found themselves in sometimes angry confrontation, for 'like the earlier nineteenth century feminists (they) opposed all legislation that put any restrictions upon women's right to work'.[40] Like their predecessors, they had a strong sense of masculine indifference to the feminine plight, and while thoroughly committed to the trade union movement, they campaigned long and hard against its misogyny.

At the same time working-class women in the Women's Co-operative Guild (WCG) were beginning to organise around other issues. Set up in the 1890s, the guild tended to attract married women and more specifically the wives of better paid artisans, of whom only a minority went out to work. 'For the greatest number,' as Margaret Llewelyn Davies said, 'their homes are their workshops'.[41] Their campaigning concerns reflected this; they are primarily known for their wide-ranging efforts to improve the lives of mothers and children. And as far as women's employment was concerned, they favoured more, not less, protective legislation, introducing a dimension that had faded from earlier campaigns: the needs of women as mothers.

Partly through the activities of the WCG, the needs of women as wives and mothers was to become a major theme in twentieth-century feminism, with a growing array of campaigns and demands, many of them around provision for children. In the nineteenth century, the women's movement drew extensively on the role of women as mothers, but primarily in the form of what became known as 'social maternalism': the conception of women as the repositories of domestic values, with a special responsibility for introducing these into the public sphere, and an obvious right to work as Poor Law Guardians, on school boards or in local councils. But it was women as symbolic rather than actual mothers that dominated the scene. 'Nineteenth-century feminists did not demand measures to improve the status and conditions of wives and mothers other than to campaign for the equal right of married women to control their own property.[42] Mothers as individuals came into their own only later and the shift, when it came, reflected both the increased presence of working-class women, and the growing acceptance of a role for the state.

By the turn of the century, we can say that feminism had become more broadly based. The movement had not transformed itself overnight into a paragon of cross-class virtue, but the single woman from the middle classes had lost her momentary centrality, while the problems of working-class women (as both workers and mothers) came into greater prominence. In the process women divided not on simple class lines, but over real and complex matters of principle. The campaign for the vote threw up difficult questions of tactics and aims; the issue of protective legislation continued a thorny one. And while class often set the terms of debate, you could not deduce the position each woman took up from a sociology of her class.

The explosion of feminism within all classes meant an unusually broad range of support for the campaign for the vote as it revitalised in the 1890s. Though still dogged by its thin end of the wedge tactic – which inclined it to accept votes for *any* women, on however restrictive a basis – the suffrage campaign soon found vocal supporters among working-class women. Women in the northern textile trades were untiring in their efforts, organising endless street meetings, collecting 31,000 signatures for a working women's petition in 1901, and constantly pressuring the TUC and Labour Party to adopt a feminist line.[43] Through much of the 1890s the Women's Co-operative Guild kept its distance from 'the goggle-eyed human ostrich, the exponent of women's rights who dresses as a man and whose bearing so nearly resembles that of a man',[44] but by the end of the 1890s was becoming more enthusiastic – despite recurring reservations over tactics that might enfranchise only single or wealthy women.[45] In a moment of relative class unity the Women's Social and Political Union (WSPU) was born, and though it came to be viewed as the organ of predominantly single, middle-class women, it emerged into being with the battle to win labour movement support. Its early meetings in the 1900s are wonderfully described in Elizabeth Robins' novel, *The Convert*, which depicts women from the working, middle and upper classes unexpectedly united under the same banners; even allowing for artistic licence, there was clearly a substantial involvement of women across all classes.[46]

But sisterhood cannot dissolve all tensions, and the suffrage movement was continually plagued by a variety of tactical issues, many of which hung on questions of class. The 1884 Reform Act had extended the parliamentary franchise to two-thirds of adult men and the line of the suffrage campaign was to call for votes for women on the same basis as they are or may be granted to men. But since the 1884 franchise still linked voting rights to householder and lodger status, it was always unclear how many working-class women would qualify for the vote: what proportion of working women could hope to qualify? and if their husbands paid the rent or rates, would the wives then count? Numerous investigations in the mid-1900s tried to establish the facts: surveys carried out by ILP branches; organised by the WCG in Leeds and Cambridge; one done in the textile town of Nelson by Selina and Robert Cooper for the WCG and the Lancashire Women Textile Workers' Representation Committee. The results seemed promising – survey after survey showed that 80 per cent, sometimes even 95 per cent – of the women enfranchised would be 'working women'.

> But in fact the figures were of doubtful worth. The areas covered were by no means representative of the whole country; certainly Nelson had an unusually high proportion of married women who did waged work outside the home. In addition the phrase 'working women' was so vague as to be almost meaningless. Certainly the opponents of women's suffrage remained unconvinced that many married women had much hope of benefitting from the bill.[47]

By the mid-1900s the choices for a working-class feminist were getting more complicated, for the labour movement was developing its political strength, and both the TUC and Labour Party discovered their alternative to votes for women in the demand for full adult suffrage. Though many working-class feminists viewed this as hypocrisy – Hannah Mitchell commented that 'we heard a lot about adult suffrage at this time from men who never seemed to have thought about it before'[48] – it was nonetheless hard to be landed with a demand that looked like 'votes for middle-class women'. Socialists said the women were putting sex above class and while working class feminists became adept in dismissing this attack, it left its mark. Ada Nield Chew was one working woman who initially fell in with the adult suffrage line, arguing that the enfranchisement of wealthy women would swamp the Labour voters among working-class men, leaving working women just as badly off as before. Others countered this, acknowledging that the long-term goal must be full womanhood suffrage, but arguing short-term support of half-way measures.[49]

It was a hard choice and had working women shifting and changing over the course of the campaign. Selina Cooper, trade unionist and suffrage organiser, remained an advocate of women's suffrage all through the debates. Ada Nield Chew moved from being an adult suffragist in the early 1900s to being a women's suffragist in the 1910s. Helen Silcock, President of the Wigan weavers, went in the opposite direction. She had led the challenge to the TUC in 1901 and 1902, arguing for a women's suffrage motion and against the evasive adult suffrage amendment. But soon after she abandoned this to throw in her lot with the adult suffrage campaign. The Women's Co-operative Guild later followed the same route, agreeing in 1905 to support *any* measure that advanced votes for women, but modifying this in 1912 to adult suffrage or nothing. The very fluidity of positions testifies to the difficulty of the choice: there was no neat formula to settle things once and for all. The intentions of those who supported adult suffrage inside the TUC and Labour Party were often deeply suspect and as G.B. Shaw commented: 'If a man owes you a sovereign and being able to pay you fifteen shillings, refuses to do so, depend upon it, ladies, he never intends to pay the lot.'[50] This said, it would be as misleading to dismiss all adult suffragists as anti-women as it would be to dismiss all women's suffragists as anti-working class. Faced with complex political choices, working-class women were almost inevitably divided among themselves, and you cannot say their class determined their ultimate positions.

What you *can* say perhaps, is that middle-class women had little patience with the issue, and that for them it was much more cut-and-dried. For Christabel Pankhurst, for example, those who hesitated over 'votes for women' were on the wrong side of the fence, and she had little sympathy with what she saw as their confusions. For working-class feminists the matter had to be more complicated and, torn as they were between their commitment to women and their commitment to their class, they could not afford such easy dismissal. Thus even those who argued vigorously in favour of votes for women and against adult suffrage recognised the seriousness of the debate; they did not presume that all those who wavered into the adult suffrage camp were thereby anti-women.

As Liddington and Norris have documented, the radical suffragists from the north of England tended to distance themselves from the WSPU once it had moved its headquarters to London and begun to detach itself from the Independent Labour Party. The shift in its political orientation, combined with the adoption of more militant methods, made the WSPU less attractive to women trade unionists and in a neat reversal of conventional stereotypes, working-class women expressed their distaste for the raucous behaviour of ladies.

> There is no class in the community who has such good reason for objecting and does so strongly object to shrieking and throwing yourself on the floor and struggling and kicking as the average working class woman, whose human dignity is very real to her. We feel we must tell you this for this reason that we are in great difficulties because our members in all parts of the Country are so outraged at the idea of taking part in such proceedings, that everywhere for the first time they are shrinking from public demonstrations. It is not the fact of demonstrations or even violence that is offensive to them, it is being mixed up and held accountable as a class for educated and upper class women who kick, shriek, bite and spit ... It is not the rioting but the *kind* of rioting.[51]

Thus in the course of 1906, the year which marked the beginning of the WSPU's policy of militant action, working class women drifted away, to find an alternative niche in the National Union of Women's Suffrage Societies, which organised the older suffrage societies under the leadership of Millicent Fawcett. Like the WSPU, its membership was overwhelmingly middle class, but at least it allowed some local autonomy and space for working-class feminists, employing both Selina Cooper and Ada Nield Chew as local organisers. Class remained a permanent sore, affecting personal relations and political choices alike, and many of the working-class activists commented on what they felt was the patronising manner of their middle-class allies. But if class influenced the ways that women campaigned for the vote, it did not deter them from action. The fact remains that against all the odds –

against the potentially divisive tactic of endorsing votes for the richer women first, against the public caricature of the movement as an exclusively middle-class concern, against the determined opposition of large sections of the labour movement – the suffrage campaign continued to command extensive working-class support. Votes for women was not just a middle-class demand.

Too much versus too little work

It was against the background of the new wave of working-class activism that the women's movement became more sensitive to the issue of too much versus too little work, and slowly and tentatively, new themes began to break through. Significantly, this was true even of Olive Schreiner's *Women and Labour*, which was in other respects typical of 'middle class' feminism.[52] Published in 1911, it served as the inspiration for many through the twentieth century, and though it echoed the pre-occupations of earlier decades, it also sounded a more qualified note.

Schreiner weighed in against what she called 'sex parasitism' and the syndrome of the fine lady. In terms derived from Pearsonian social dynamics (applying the findings of biology to analysis of the social world), but also reminiscent of Mary Wollstonecraft, she denounced this creature as 'the most deadly microbe which can make its appearance on the surface of any social organism'.[53] Like Wollstonecraft, she argued that women in the upper classes had always played this role, but only recently had it become an option for the majority of women. Men might like us to be lowly parasites, but they would never seriously countenance this if it left them to do all our work. As long as woman's work was arduous, we could rest assured that she would have to do it. In the nineteenth century the oppressive existence of the 'fine lady' was reserved for a 'fortunate' few.

But by the twentieth century labour-saving technology was beginning to threaten the very basis of household labour. Traditional responsibilities for baking, sewing, educating the children, were being taken from women's hands; new industries had arisen which could substitute for household labour. And in consequence sex parasitism was becoming a real possibility, not just for the upper, but for the middle classes – in fifty years' time for working-class women as well. If women were to save themselves from this new oppression, they must find work. 'Give us labour and the training which fits us for labour' was to be Schreiner's rallying cry, a call that echoed a long tradition of feminist campaigns.

Yet even as she wrote this, she felt it was inadequate. When she published her book, she prefaced it with what is almost an apology, stressing that it was only a tiny fragment of a larger whole. Taken in isolation the argument could mislead. Sex parasitism was not the only problem for women; we must also remember 'the work woman has done and still does in the modern world, and the gigantic evils which arise from the fact that her labour, especially domestic labour, often the most wearisome and unending known to any section of the human race, is not adequately recognised or recompensed.'[54]

Olive Shreiner's experiences in Africa – and indeed her sensitivity to the conditions of working-class life – left her uneasy with the undiluted cry for work. Even in the 'fragment' she indicated this, noting that 'probably much more than half the world's most laborious and ill-paid labour is still performed by women, from tea pickers and cocoa tenders in India and the islands, to the washerwomen, cooks, and drudging labouring men's wives, who, in addition to the sternest and most unending toil, throw in their child-bearing as a little addition.'[55] She knew about the 'landlady, now about to give birth to her ninth child', who had to carry heavy coal scuttles up from the cellar and busy herself with bending over hot fires; the 'haggard, work-worn woman and mother who irons (her husband's) shirts'; 'the woman, who, on hands or knees, at tenpence a day scrubs the floors'. Using such examples to attack men who have the nerve to deny us work because we are 'too delicate', yet the hypocrisy to thrive on the back-breaking drudgery of female labour, she also confirmed her anxieties about the limits of her argument. For some women (primarily middle class) the problem was too little work; for others (primarily working class) the problem was too much.

This theme was to be explicitly developed in Mabel Atkinson's *The Economic Foundations of the Women's Movement*, a tract published by the Fabian Women's Group in 1914.[56] In one of the clearest attempts of the time to define the class character of the women's movement, she argued that women were affected in different ways by the onslaughts of the industrial revolution: 'to put it shortly, parasitism became the fate of the middle-class woman, ruthless exploitation that of the working-class woman.'[57] When the women's movement sprang into life in the 1860s, it was 'on the whole a demand of elderly unmarried women for the right to freer activities, as the alternative to an impracticable ideal of marriage and motherhood for every woman'.[58] As a result it could see no difference between 'the right of a woman to be a doctor and the right of a woman to work underground in a mine', and vigorously opposed any attempt at factory legislation.

The result, she argued, had been a women's movement divided into two sections:

> the movement of the middle-class women who are revolting against their exclusion from human activity and insisting, firstly, on their right to education, which is now practically conceded on all sides; secondly, on their right to earn a livelihood for themselves, which is rapidly being won; and thirdly, on their right to share in the control of government, the point around which the fight is now most fiercely raging. These women are primarily rebelling against the sex-exclusiveness of men and regard independence and the right to work as the most valuable privilege to be striven for.
>
> On the other hand there are the women of the working classes, who have been faced with a totally different problem and who naturally react in a different way. Parasitism has never been forced on them. Even when the working-class woman does not earn her own living in the world of industry – through practically all the unmarried girls of the working classes do so – her activities at home are so unending, and she subconsciously feels so important and so valuable, that she has never conceived of herself as useless and shut out from human interests, as was the parasitic middle-class woman. What the woman of the proletariat feels as her grievance is that her work is too long and too monotonous, the burden laid upon her is too heavy. Moreover, in her case that burden is due to the capitalistic exploitation resulting from the injustice of our social system. It is not due, or not, at least to any considerable extent, to the fact that the men of her class shut her out from gainful occupation. Therefore among the working-class women there is less sex-con-sciousness ... The working woman feels her solidarity with the men of her class rather than their antagonism to her. The reforms that she demands are not independence and the

right to work, but rather protection against the unending burden of toil which has been laid upon her.'[59]

The description has the heart-felt appeal of what was nonetheless a half-truth, for the split was hardly as stark as it suggests. On the issue of the right to work versus protective legislation the divisions had been more complex and working-class women had often exhibited as sharp a sense of 'sex-consciousness' as anyone could wish – the radical suffragists we have come across certainly had their fair share. But it was because she felt poised at a moment of convergence that Mabel Atkinson could exaggerate previous divisions, for *now*, she claimed, working-class women were beginning to see that 'their interests are not altogether safe in the hands of the men',[60] and in particular not their interests as mothers; *now* middle-class women were at last noting the limits of wage labour, and instead of glorying in their alternatives to marriage, were struggling to combine the needs of motherhood with those of work. The two classes could finally converge on the battle for 'state endowment', campaigning not just for jobs and wages, but for family allowances to cover their years as mothers.

When this pamphlet was published, women were mobilised not just around the suffrage societies, but in a number of over-lapping organisations that engaged directly with the tensions of gender and class. The Women's Co-operative Society had gone on from strength to strength, from a mere 51 branches in 1889 to 611 in 1914, and despite its formal links with the male co-operative movement, it had pursued a determinedly feminist line. Inside the co-operative societies, it had fought – and by 1914 won – the principle of equal pay to their male and female workers, while on the explosive issue of divorce legislation it had refused to moderate its support for easier divorce. As the only organisation of working class women to give evidence to the Royal Commission on Divorce Law Reform (set up in 1909), the WCG argued a cogent case for giving working-class families the same chances of divorce as those with money, and when the Co-operative Union (which included a powerful Catholic lobby) expressed its disapproval, the Guild chose to relinquish its annual grant of £400 rather than abandon its position.[61]

The Women's Trade Union League, under the powerful leadership of Mary Macarthur, continued to operate as a focus for the unionisation of women, but after its about-turn on the issue of protective legislation, had avoided direct conflict with male trade unionism. Of course many unions dismissed the work of the League. Indeed it was partly their continuing exclusionary practices that provoked the formation in 1906 of a National Federation of Women Workers (NFWW), for in those trades where male trade unions had proved unco-operative, women had formed their own, usually tiny, female societies, and the object of the Federation was to strengthen their hand. But even in the organisation of separate women's unions, the WTUL and NFWW were not in the business of confrontation with the labour movement. Thus when the First World War broke out and the employment of women in men's jobs threw up fears of 'dilution', Mary Macarthur and the NFWW went out of their way to calm the spirits of skilled engineers. 'The understood, if not always expressed, basis of co-operation was that the women would promise to give up their jobs when the men came home, that the men would support the women's claim to a living wage in the meantime, and that both sides would press for decent conditions and for reasonable hours of work.'[62]

The Women's Labour League (WLL) was also launched in 1906, with the remit of encouraging the labour representation of women in Parliament and local councils, and a particular orientation towards the conditions of working-class women. This proved more vulnerable than the WCG to the pressures to fall in behind its 'fraternal' organisation, and on issues to do with female economic independence, was wary of challenging the role of the male bread-winner. Split over protective legislation, and the right of married women to work, the League tended to compromise with labour movement prejudice. Thus, for example, when the WCG led a campaign in 1913 for the payment direct to mothers of the new maternity benefit introduced by the Liberal Government's National Insurance Act, the WLL withheld its support, noting that

> on account of the strong feeling raised by the matter, far more important questions might be overlooked ... We did not oppose payment to the mother, but we felt that if it caused difficulties and delays in administering it, it was not worth so much as to be of vital importance.[63]

The differences between these organisations was not a matter of the class of their members: it was not that middle-class women made gender their priority while working-class women united with their class. The organisations overlapped in membership, with the same names cropping up between the Women's Co-operative Guild, the Women's Trade Union League, the National Federation of Women Workers, the Women's Industrial Council, the Women's Labour League, and Mabel Atkinson's own base, the Fabian Women's Group. Of these, it was the WCG and NFWW that spoke most directly as organisations of working-class women, but even here middle-class women had a major role: Margaret Llewelyn Davies, so crucial in the growth and radicalisation of the former, was the daughter of a rector; while Mary Macarthur, the inspiration of the latter, was the daughter of a well-established shop-keeper. If the women who worked through these bodies often spoke with muted voice on issues of female economic independence and the right to work, it was because their route through the institutions of the labour movement imposed major constraints; if the WCG then emerged as one of the more forceful voices of women's interests, it was partly because it held more aloof from union affairs.

Within this plethora of bodies, it was the Fabian Women's Group that was most unreserved in its commitment to a woman's right to work, but as Mabel Atkinson's comments indicate, it was the proposal for state endowment of women that was supposed to cut the Gordian knot. However much class had affected feminist debates, however much relations with the unions and Labour Party strained positions over married women's employment, the place for protective legislation, the equal right of women to work, surely under this banner all could unite?

Her instincts were right when she picked on motherhood as the issue of the future. After the war, maternity was to become the basis for a realignment within the (much reduced) feminist movement, a basis which nearly – though in the end not quite – overcame the class differences she outlined. In the inter-war years the submerged issue of too much versus too little work came out into the open; the problem of female poverty was more fully aired; the notion of the feminist as a middle-class woman in pursuit of a job was radically overturned.

The 'New Feminism'

In the 1920s people talked of a 'new feminism' which took maternity as the central issue, dwarfing the previous demands for a woman's right to work. If it suggests complete novelty, the term is misleading – when Mary Wollstonecraft appealed to women to resume their rights and responsibilities, it was the work of mothering she had most in mind. Women as mothers had never dropped from view, but 'what was new in the feminism of the inter-war years was the emphasis on the needs of mothers as individuals, rather than on social maternalism.'[64] The new generation of feminists now saw their ancestors as carried away by their overwhelming need for work. Too engrossed in refuting the male cry that women are 'merely' wives and mothers, they had lost themselves in proving that women could be workers too; in the process they had almost forgotten that women still had children.

The 'new feminists' fought instead on the platform of motherhood, taking up a wide range of welfare issues. Women should have access to contraceptive advice and facilities – not so much to help them choose childlessness, but to enable them to decide for themselves how many children and when. Once pregnant, they should get state support in the form of ante-natal clinics, free milk, community midwives. And as mothers, they should receive cash payments from the state – the 'family endowment' demand pushed most forcefully by Eleanor Rathbone.[65] The state should pay for feeding and clothing a child, and more than this, for feeding and clothing a mother. It was all very well to say women needed jobs, but how did this help the woman confined at home to care for her children? What she needed was maintainence during her years of child rearing.

The arguments were often couched in class terms, and they drew on the evidence collected by the Fabian Women's Group and Co-operative Women's Guild: Maud Pember Reeves' *Round About A Pound A Week*, published in 1913, and Margaret Llewelyn Davies' *Maternity: Letters From Working Women*, published in 1915.[66] When Dora Russell, for example, became involved in the campaign for birth control facilities, she explained her commitment in terms of the *working-class* mother:

> I began to wonder if the feminists had not been running away from the central issue of women's emancipation. Would women ever be truly free and equal with men until we had liberated mothers? Demanding equality and vote, women in the Labour movement had argued that there should now be no distinction between men's and women's questions, a view which I had more or less accepted until I came up against this

issue of maternity. What rights had the working-class mother? Dependent on her man's income, she yet had no claim to a share of it; she must bear and attempt to feed and care for every child born to her; left in ignorance of the functioning of her own body, she must accept with gratitude the charitable help from the maternity clinics and the patronage of health visitors and the middle-class ladies who came to 'weigh the babies' at the clinic sessions. Yet was not this woman, and her children, the very foundation stone and future of our race and nation? How come then that our religious leaders and politicians could despise, neglect and oppress her?[67]

The oppression of working-class women was seen as encapsulated in their conditions as mothers, and if feminists ran away from this they evacuated the main arena of struggle. They might even delude themselves that the battles were already won: that 'there should now be no distinction between men's and women's questions'; that getting involved in the marginal territory of 'women's questions' would undermine their credibility as political activists. This fear was indeed widely expressed among women in both Labour and Communist parties in the inter-war years. But in giving in to this, Russell argued, women were acting out a class view of gender oppression. They were assuming that exclusion from work or politics were the only problems, and trying to solve these by denying themselves as women.

For feminists who had fought long and hard against the idea that they were made to have children and nothing else, these ideas sounded dangerous stuff. Instead of challenging conventional male and female roles, they seemed to wallow in the difference, abandoning all pretence of sexual equality. How could you fight for equality if you defined women primarily through their reproductive role? 'What has feminism to do with mothers?' asked a bewildered (woman) reviewer of Dora Russell's *Hypatia* in 1925![68]

In principle the gap could have been reduced. Those who argued for family endowment also argued for the right to jobs and equal pay and at no point suggested that women should be *only* wives and mothers. Eleanor Rathbone, for example, based her case for family endowment on the principle of female independence, attacking the assumptions of the 'family wage' which forced mothers and children to depend on the generosity of their men. The fiction that male earnings were meant to maintain the entire family justified higher pay for men than for women, forcing single women into poverty wages and giving single men an unfair bonus. For married women things were just as bad: wages were never adjusted to the real size of a family, so those with more children were left in destitution. And even where income was adequate, women should not have to rely on a male wage. 'A man has no right to keep half the world in purgatory because he enjoys playing redeemer to his own wife and children.'[69]

There was meat enough in this to satisfy an equal rights feminist: it argued for equal pay for workers of either sex, and an independent income for women confined to the home. But still the emphasis on women as mothers was felt as a dangerous turn and feminists soon divided into different camps. Protective legislation was again a focal point for disagreement, for clearly, this new emphasis on maternity could imply a powerful case for additional protection. Since women are the ones to carry and care for children, they may well need different laws from men.

Up to the mid-1920s the divisions over protective legislation had continued broadly in the pattern set by late nineteenth century debates. The Women's Trade Union League, the Women's Co-operative Guild, and of course the labour movement in general were for it. The descendants of the suffrage societies – The National Union of Societies for Equal Citizenship (NUSEC) which was formed in 1919 out of the National Union of Women's Suffrage Societies, and the Women's Freedom League – continued to argue against. In 1926 a new body was set up (of both socialist and non-socialist feminists) which declared war on any legislation that discriminated on the grounds of sex. The Open Door Council aimed at total equality inside the labour force:

> To secure that a woman shall be free to work and protected as a worker on the same terms as a man, and that legislation and regulations dealing with conditions and hours, payment, entry and training shall be based upon the nature of the work and not upon the sex of the worker: and to secure for a woman, irrespective of marriage and childbirth, the right at all times to decide whether or not she shall engage in paid work and to ensure that no legislation or regulations shall deprive her of this right.[70]

'Irrespective of marriage and childbirth' – quite a challenge to these new currents that insisted on the major difference that marriage and childbirth made.

NUSEC called a special conference to assess its response and re-affirmed its own long-standing opposition to protective legislation. But in its next annual conference this decision was reversed. Eleanor Rathbone secured a narrow margin of 81 votes to 80 to bring NUSEC more in line with the labour movement position. For the first time, a major bastion of 'middle-class feminism' had been won over to protective legislation. And as if to underline the revised consensus, a counter-motion that would have relegated campaigns over birth control and family endowment to secondary importance was simultaneously defeated. Those who defined themselves primarily in terms of equal political and legal rights – the 'me-too feminists' as Rathbone called them – resigned their seats on the NUSEC council. Women continued to fight on the platform of equal rights, combatting the marriage bar in teaching and the civil service, fighting for equal pay. But the predominant issues of these inter-war years were to do with the conditions of mothers and children.

Women as workers: women as mothers

As far as the relationship of class and gender is concerned, this might look like a major advance. Feminism's identification with middle-class professional women had been shattered, and the working-class mother had emerged as the new symbol of oppressed womanhood. Women in the labour movement organisations – the Co-operative Women's Guild, the Women's Labour League, the Standing Joint Committee of Working Women's Industrial Organisations – were focussing their campaigns on the needs of women and children, and now they were being joined by their more exclusively middle-class sisters. The blindspot had been illuminated. The notion that liberation meant the freedom to compete on equal terms with men had been revealed in all its inadequacies. For most women, equal competition was a farce, and at last the movement had admitted this.

But in fact it was a case of damned if you do and damned if you don't. In the nineteenth century feminism was most typically concerned with women as workers; now it was most typically concerned with women as mothers. What was needed then (as it is needed now) was a way of cutting through such oppositions, for women are both, regardless of their class. But the battle for women as workers had been too closely associated with the struggles of middle-class women, and was now discredited as such. Going on about equal rights only revealed your class position. Invoking the name of the working-class mother, feminists reversed their position. A mirror image, unfortunately, rarely corrects the vision. The fact that working-class women *also* needed the right to work – a point so forcibly made by the radical suffragists before the war – dropped from view. In the increased class awareness of these years, those who continued to campaign around women's right to a job were all too easily dismissed as the single, childless, professional women.

As Denise Riley has shown in her *War in the Nursery*, this meant that feminism was paralysed in the face of the later pronatalist climate of opinion.[71] In the 1930s and '40s the low birth rate was causing considerable alarm. Women were increasingly exhorted to realise their potential as mothers – four children each was regarded as a desirable norm! The woman in the home, the man in the factory: each fulfilling their duties to the race. It was a deeply anti-feminist perspective, yet the women's movement put up a surprisingly feeble defence.

In the late 1940s the wartime nurseries were being closed down, the progressive potential in the wartime employment of married women was being dissipated, and yet feminist organisations spoke with muted tones in stemming this tide. When all around were celebrating the duties and delights of motherhood, when Royal Commissions agonised over the declining birth rate, when pronatalist thinking came to such prominence in popular culture, why did feminism keep so quiet? Why couldn't the feminists at least speak out for the working mother? Because their self-definition in the inter-war years left them ill-prepared for this attack.

Predictably, the one body to speak out against pronatalism was the Open Door International. In its first International Conference in 1938, it had questioned the trend in dictatorships and democracies alike, arguing that even the more progressive versions could still confirm age-old prejudices about the role and duties of women. Ten years on its worst fears had been confirmed: 'the woman is being increasingly looked on not as an independent personality, a complete human being but rather as a medium for the production of children.'[72] In principle this grouping offered one possible focus for resistance, but Open Door feminism had become too closely identified with the needs of the single, childless, professional woman for this to work in practice. Its voice was isolated and easily dismissed.

Well into the 1940s, working women's organisations still felt they must fight for the needs and status of the mother, against the invidious distortions of the old 'equal rightsers'. As the Standing Joint Committee of Working Women's Organisations put it:

> Some of the earlier feminist propaganda, with its emphasis on equality in fields of work previously closed to women merely on grounds of sex, tended to perpetuate the idea that the work of a home and children is of less importance than work outside the home, a less eligible career than most others, and may have helped to influence some women against motherhood. This attitude was found chiefly in middle-class and professional groups and is probably less usual today than it was twenty five years ago. Our working women's organisations have never accepted it, and, while insisting on the right of women to follow the work of their choice, they have worked for many years for a better status for the work of the wife and mother in the home.[73]

Wanting to distance themselves from what they saw as the emphasis of the earlier women's movement, such organisations abandoned the weapons that might have helped distinguish their commitment to working-class maternity from the more dangerous preoccupations of pronatalist thought. Their own demands were too closely mirrored in the recommendations of those who worried about population decline, but however ill at ease they felt in this new climate they lacked the language with which to attack it.

Feminists were trying to throw off what they saw as the legacy of class, but found it still forced them into a dangerous polarity. In early years the women's movement *had* generalised too much from middle-class experience, and in its overtures to working-class women had too often reproduced the stereotypes of the time. But when later activists tried to reverse the trend they shifted too far in an opposite direction, losing some of the real insights of the previous generations. The problem was a hard one: it is never an easy matter to combine the needs of women as workers with their needs as mothers, and again and again we fall into campaigns which focus on the one to the exclusion of the other. But this difficult task was further complicated by the impact of class on the politics of women.

As this and previous episodes illustrate, the key problem in the history of the women's movement is not that it was exclusively for privileged women, nor that it evaded all issues of class. Even at the zenith of middle-class dominance – in the 1860s, '70s and '80s, feminists took on questions of wider significance and many of them regarded the conditions of 'industrial women' as a crucial area of struggle. By the 1890s a new wave of working-class feminism had arisen to create some troubled interludes in the battle for the vote, while the growing importance of the labour movement in general was reflected in the pre-war activities of women of all classes. In the aftermath of the First World War feminism tried to revise itself in the light of working-class experience and shake off once and for all the images of the single, professional woman. Class issues *were* recognised and the women's movement strove towards a fuller understanding of the oppression of *all* women.

But *recognising* class does not solve the problems and over a range of difficult questions women took up a variety of stances. The choices they faced were sometimes tactical ones: whether, for example, to support *any* extension of votes to women, on however restricted a basis? They sometimes involved major matters of emphasis: whether to highlight conditions of employment or to focus on conditions for mothers; whether to work through female unions or campaign for change through the state? They often implied competing theories of women's oppression: whether more competition would help or would hinder; whether unions are the problem or the capitalist market? They inevitably involved different perceptions of the future ideal: whether women should be the same as men or develop their strengths in a separate sphere? And often enough they were a combination of questions of tactics and matters of principle, for when feminists were working to secure an alliance with men in the labour movement, they differed both over how far you need to compromise and over what the ultimate goals should be. On virtually all these matters there were valid arguments for opposing positions, and in the event it was rarely middle-class women lined up exclusively on the one side with working-class women on the other.

But as each new issue arose it often became codified in class terms, and when differences of opinion got translated into differences of class, the real complexity of the issues at stake was often denied. At moments of too little class consciousness, class limited women's perception of the complexities: some of the episodes over protective legislation or the battle for the vote serve as examples here. But too little consciousness then alternated with too much, and the one could prove as bad as the other. Once a particular feminist line got identified as 'middle class' and another as 'working class' – as when employment issues were identified with the former and maternity issues with the latter – then the task of integrating what can seem conflicting needs became much more difficult. Feminism cannot afford over-simplification, but the tensions of class often pushed it this way. It is in this sense, rather than the more straightforward one of dominance by middle-class women, that class has troubled the course of women's movement politics. Feminism operates within the confines of a class society and has not escaped its pressures.

5 When Sisters Fall Out

If class was an ever present sub-text through the early years of feminism, it was later to be written up large – and in terms that provoked much anger. The Women's Liberation Movement emerged in the late 1960s in a ferment of radical ideas, drawing many of its supporters from a prior or continuing involvement in socialist/communist groups. The engagement with socialism was formative and a minor flurry in the first year of national organisation indicates some of the flavour. When the first national conference was held in 1970, it set up a Women's National Co-ordinating Committee, which was then dominated by organisationally adept women from existing left groups. Degenerating subsequently into 'sectarian squabbles between the different left factions represented',[1] the committee was disbanded at the next annual conference, leaving a legacy of distaste for formal structures – and a healthy suspicion of the organised left.

In these early years, class was often put to pejorative purposes by those socialists who saw feminism as 'bourgeois', and while women in socialist groupings waged lengthy battles inside their organisations to dislodge such ideas, they too took class as the marker of 'serious' action. Thus commenting on their involvement in the London Night-Cleaners' Campaign in 1970 and 1971, the (Trotskyist) London Socialist Woman Group contrasted their own privileged relationship to class struggle with what they saw as the individualism and reformism of non-socialist women:

In many ways the fact that we are a *socialist* woman's group made all the difference, in that we took part in the campaign because we understood why it was important; in contrast to the very individualistic approach taken by some 'a-political' women's groups who went out leafletting because it was a 'fun thing to do', who found it 'all rather abstract' and 'had difficulty relating to it' ... If the slogan 'Women Unite' is to mean anything, it should mean that women of all classes must recognise that the oppression of working-class women is the most fundamental and unite with them in *their* struggles for liberation – which can't of course be realised without a complete change in the structure of society – rather than expecting the bringing of non-class issues to working women to solve anything.[2]

The idea that 'working women' would have little time for many of the themes of women's liberation was a prevalent note: four years on, and in much more denunciatory vein, the (Maoist) Union of Women for Liberation claimed that, 'Working class women had long, rightly rejected the feminist, petty-bourgeois-oriented women's liberation movement whose members seek, not emancipation for all women, but "solutions" for their own, individual problems.'[3]

Attacks like the latter could be easily shrugged off, but in its less extreme versions the argument played on what were widespread anxieties within the movement, for the predominance of ex-student, white collar and professional women was often noted as a weakness – by socialist and non-socialist alike. But when class was used to put feminism in its place, its arguments had to be rebutted, and women of both persuasions set to work on their counter-critique. Dislodging class from its previous centrality became one of the budding feminist's first tasks, as those who had often learnt their politics through the conflicts between capital and labour now had to transform their vision in the light of conflicts between women and men.

The relationship between feminist and socialist politics was to remain a major issue, and it formed positions in a variety of ways. It meant that links between the women's movement and what was seen as conventional class politics was a recurrent cause for concern: reflected on the one hand in a growing suspicion of left groups but on the other in an almost universal rejection of careerist or 'bourgeois' feminism. Activists in the movement shared a commitment to the struggles of working-class women, and accounts of the early years give due weight (or perhaps considering the reality, undue weight) to the impact of such struggle: while noting the influence of student radicalism, or the spread of feminist ideas from America, they often give pride of place to the self-organisation of working-class women.[4]

In 1968 a group of fishermen's wives from Hull organised a campaign against the appalling safety conditions on the fishing trawlers. Later in the same year women sewing machinists in the Ford factory at Dagenham went on an historic strike for the upgrading of their work, and though their full demands were not to be met for another fifteen years, their action was an important influence on the Labour Government's decision to introduce an Equal Pay Act in 1970. In the late summer of 1970, May Hobbs, a long-standing working-class militant who had worked for twelve years as a night-cleaner, formed the Cleaners' Action Group to campaign for union recognition and higher pay; women from the London Women's Liberation Workshop, as well as women from socialist groups, joined the picket lines in solidarity.[5] In 1972 women occupied their shoe factory at Fakenham in Norfolk, setting up what was to be a precursor of a number of women workers' co-operatives; again there was supportive action from feminists. The links could be tenuous and mutually suspicious; the prominence of such moments in histories of the movement reflect as much the significance feminists attached to them as any sustained experience of united action. But it is a striking index of the concerns of the contemporary women's movement that such struggles were viewed as a crucial part of what women's liberation was about. (Perhaps more cynically, it testifies to an undercurrent of fear that feminism might after all be 'bourgeois', and a relief when the evidence helped dispel such doubts.)

The Women's Liberation Movement in Britain had little time for any 'women-into-top-jobs' approach, and early conferences rang with tales, not of women kept out of boardrooms, but of single mothers running the gauntlet of the DHSS cohabitation rules, of married women trapped at home by the demands of husband, children and housework, of manual workers ghettoised into typically ill-paid jobs. The first four demands formulated in 1970 may have spoken the traditional language of equal rights, but the way these were justified went far beyond;

Equal pay

We have to understand *why* we don't have equal pay. It's always been said that a woman's place is in the home. We don't want to do equal work and housework as well. We don't want to do equal work when it's shitwork. Equal pay means not just the same money for the same work, but also means recognising how many women work not because they want to, but because they *have* to, either for money or for friends. Equal pay is the first step not just to more money, but to control over how, why, and for whom we work.

Equal education and opportunity

We don't want to demand an education equally as bad as that of men – we want equal resources, not equal repression. We want to fight for real education, to make our own jobs and opportunities.

24-hour nurseries

We need somewhere for the kids, but we have to choose as to whether the kids will be kept out of the way or given their own space, and whether, freed from children, we just manage to survive through working or make the time to discover who stops us from living.

Free contraception and abortion on demand

We want to be free to choose when and how many kids to have, if any. We have to fight for control over our own bodies, for even the magic pill or (in case of mistakes) abortion on demand only gives us the freedom to get into a real mess without any visible consequences. We still can't talk of sex as anything but a joke or a battle-ground.[6]

Women's liberation was self-consciously grass-roots and anti-elitist, and though much of this derived from a critique of how men did things, and sometimes more specifically how *socialist* men did things, it was also about refusing the hierarchies of a class-ridden society. When women set up consciousness-raising groups, questioned the necessity for formal structures, challenged the place of leaders and stars, they were primarily rejecting the practices of male discussion. But they were also tackling the tensions of class. Whatever had happened in the past (and most of us did not yet have a clue) this women's movement was not going to be about privileged women: not top women clamouring for a space among top men, but *all* women finding a voice through which to speak their oppression.

The exuberance of sisterhood could spell tremendous release for those who had been engaged in socialist politics: release from the constraints of thinking only in class terms; release from the fears that feminism was 'bourgeois'; release from the task of making the tea. And for those who had been dogged by the ambiguities in being both middle class and socialist, it was part of the appeal of women's politics that it seemed to sweep these away. Speaking for myself, I can remember the extraordinary relief of discovering that I too was oppressed, that no longer the 'maid in the attic of someone else's movement'[7] I was now a fully fledged proprietor in my own right. It sounds absurd – who wants to be oppressed? – but the power of feminist politics was that it arose from personal experience and compared with the more theoretical, perhaps altruistic, basis on which I adhered to a socialist politics, this seemed so much more real. The women's movement was about *us* not *them* – and to this extent at least, was quite properly immune to those who dismissed its supporters as unrepresentative and middle class. Let no one dare tell us that middle-class women had no problems of their own!

Thus while the pre-history of many feminists in socialist or radical politics kept class on the agenda, the experience of women's groups and women's conferences helped create a different climate. Some of the first campaigns were around what we can loosely call ideology: the demonstrations at the Miss World contests, for example, which challenged the way women were exposed as sex objects for the male gaze. The very language of *oppression* (rather than exploitation) reinforced the point, for it drew attention to the way that *all* women, regardless of their position in the economy, are exposed to the same humiliations, degradations and contempt. The subordination of women was not just a matter of work and pay and as consciousness-raising groups enabled women to speak out their needs, a vision of an entirely different kind of life came into view. Women's oppression had its material base, but it also fed on complex relations of submission, self-denial, martyrdom and guilt; and in experiments in new forms of communal living, in tortured discussions on possessiveness and jealousy, in confident assertions that marriage must be abolished and the nuclear family must go, the contemporary women's movement put into practice its claim that 'the personal *is* political'.

Being a feminist could imply then an extraordinary juxtaposition of activities, some of which were continuous with older-style 'class' politics, some of which must have seemed totally bizarre. You might be doing night duty on the office cleaners' pickets; campaigning for money to set up a nursery; disrupting a Miss World competition with smoke bombs and bags of flour; arguing with men about who does the housework; struggling with yourself over who sleeps with whom. And being political in every aspect of your life could impose tremendous strains, for as Mica Nava recounts from her experience in the Belsize Lane Women's Liberation Group in the early 1970s, it meant that everything you did was available for comment.

> ... our households were among a number of people who gathered on Hampstead Heath each fine Sunday to picnic and play volley-ball together. These gatherings were significant because the truth about the division of child-care within our living units was made quite public. Both men and women were, in a sense, on trial. If young children ran on to the volley-ball pitch and disrupted the game by crying for comfort from their mothers rather than their fathers or 'other friendly adults', we could feel quite exposed. This sort of occurrence seemed an almost shameful demonstration of our inability to progress beyond the stage of consciousness-raising.[8]

This of course was precisely the side of the women's movement that some socialists could find so distressing, for what had this to do with class?

For women involved in the movement too, there could be recurring doubts – not so such about whether any of the activities engaged in by feminists were off the point, but about what might be left out. Socialist feminists remained uneasy over how to relate the politics of gender with the politics of class, and this was often expressed in a priority given to work among women trade unionists. Interestingly, the pendulum seemed to have swung back again, and while in the inter-war years it was maternity that was regarded as the key issue in the conditions of working-class women, by the 1970s it was employment. The change partly reflected reality, for most working-class women, whether married or not, now had jobs – many of them in poorly unionised, and nearly all in low-paid sectors. But the shift also revealed a tendency towards simplistic equations: if you thought about class, then you thought about women at work.

Workers or housewives? old questions in a new language

One of the developments that gave expression to this concern was the Working Women's Charter Campaign, launched in 1974 after the London Trades Council approved a ten-point Working Women's Charter that had been drawn up by feminists inside the Communist Party. The demands related to women at work but were not exclusively about employment; they called for equal pay, training and opportunities at work, a national minimum wage, and eighteen weeks maternity leave at full pay; but they also called for free nurseries, free contraception and abortion on demand, improved family allowances, and an end to all legal and bureaucratic impediments to equality. At one level the campaign was extraordinarily successful, for it soon won national validation from a variety of unions (including the AUEW, NALGO, NUPE, NUJ, CPSA, ACTT) and local branch support from more. Its activities were undoubtedly influential in the subsequent formulation of TUC policy on women, which by the end of the 1970s had a relatively impressive (if largely paper) commitment to most of these aims.

The appeal of such a campaign (particularly to socialist feminists) was obvious, as Jeannette Mitchell reflected in 1977:

> Socialist feminists were attracted to the Charter Campaign because they saw it as a way of making the ideas of the thus far inward-looking Women's Liberation Movement relevant to working-class women. Because the Charter focussed on what were seen as material pre-requisites of women's liberation the Charter was seen as a way of raising basic questions by tackling practicalities: nurseries, abortion, working conditions and so on. It seemed to provide a way of organising around specific issues – like nurseries – in a way which gave these struggles a context, a way of talking about and linking up all the problems women face. We argued that 'working women' means *all* women, whether or not they are engaged in waged labour, and saw the Charter as a way of linking up women at work and in the home. In practice, however, these assumptions have not proved viable.[9]

The Charter Campaign quickly became a forum for heated if obscure debates between women from a variety of left groupings (the quote from the Union of Women for Liberation is taken from a wordy pamphlet they produced in 1975, denouncing the 'anti-working class politics' and 'bureaucratic manoeuvring' of the Trotskyites who they claimed controlled the campaign). Conferences often focussed on amending the Charter to bring it more in line with the theoretical persuasions of competing groups, while the National Co-ordinating Group had an over-representation of women from the organised left as compared to the activists in the campaign as a whole.

And in its conception of politics, the campaign tended to draw on the style of the labour rather than the women's movement. It put its efforts into securing official support at national level rather than holding grass-roots discussion to win people over; it emphasised co-operative action by men and women at the expense of autonomous organisation of women with the result that local groups were not only mixed but usually dominated by men; and it reproduced a 'male trade union definition of "working class" ' in which only women in unskilled manual jobs were regarded as legitimate targets.[10] Some of these problems were perhaps inescapable, for if the point of the campaign was to win over trade union support, it had to work within existing structures. But the failure of intent was nonetheless revealing: not so much a partnership between gender and class, but a marriage which had the former bowing to the latter.

Vigorously opposed to the Charter, and indeed to any initiatives that sought to improve women's access to the labour market, was the Wages For Housework Campaign. Under the redoubtable leadership of Selma James, this was a campaign with superb propaganda skills, and it captured much more media attention than its (many) critics within the women's movement felt it deserved. Issues of WIRES, the movement's monthly internal newsletter, were punctuated through the later 1970s with complaints of newspaper reports that seemed to assume Wages for Housework *was* the women's movement, of radio interviews by the group that helped reinforce this impression, of demonstrations where their loudspeaker equipment drowned out other chants. Grounded in a version of revolutionary socialism that saw the refusal of work as the major challenge to capital, the campaign set itself firmly against what Mariarosa Dalla Costa dismissed as the 'myth of liberation through work'.[11] Getting women out of the household into the factory or office was not liberation but defeat; getting women into unions was capitulation to the very institutions that held down workers' power. The real power of women lay in wresting a sphere of autonomy and control – as the title of Dalla Costa's inspirational essay put it, *The Power of Women and the Subversion of the Community* – and calling on the state to pay wages for housework became then part of this project.

The argument was twofold. Women should refuse the ideological clap-trap that binds them to their homes: if you have to work then you'd better be paid. (It was this that provided the theoretical bridge between Wages for Housework and the associated English Collective of Prostitutes, for with their vision cleared of romantic rubbish, prostitutes see sex as work and they expect to be paid.) Housewives should sweep away the delusions of romance and duty, but in doing so they should beware of that alternative illusion of freedom through jobs. No point fleeing the domestic tyrant if you then end up in the hands of the capitalist boss. Demanding a wage for their housework, their childcare, their sexual services, women should carve out a niche for themselves beyond the mind-bending disciplines of the factory or office; refusing the direct command of capital, they should begin to assert their power.

The notion that housework was work, and that in their domestic labour women serviced not only men but capitalism too, was widely canvassed in the movement as a whole: a popular poster of the time showed an assembly line of housewives, feeding and packaging their men for return to the factory gates. Outside the Wages For Housework campaign related arguments surfaced in what is known as the domestic labour debate – an episode since derided as subservience to marxist logic, but important then in shifting the balance of discussion.[12] The emphasis here was on extending the scope of marxist value theory, showing how the unpaid labour women do in the home can feed into the profits of capital. Exploitation, it was argued, takes place at home as well as on the factory bench: an argument that seemed to shed light on the hidden army of housewives, bringing them into the glare of capitalist power. But few of those engaged in *this* debate were prepared to go along with the political conclusions of wages for housework, for payment for domestic labour seemed to institutionalise women's position in the home. As the demand for free twenty-four hour nurseries implied, most feminists at this point were more keen on the idea of socialising housework and childcare, and/or making sure that the men did their share. From 1972 onwards there were repeated attempts to introduce wages for housework as an additional women's movement demand, and year after year the initiative was frustrated. The campaign became a thorn in the flesh, its single-minded interventions so divisive and disruptive that by late 1970s WIRES was refusing to publish its material. Wages For Housework since developed in almost total isolation from the rest of women's movement activities.

Yet if we take these two campaigns in juxtaposition – the Working Women's Charter Campaign and Wages For Housework – what is interesting is that both could claim a legitimacy based on their greater understanding of the predicament of working-class women, and yet that each was the mirror of the other. The one focussed on women as waged workers, agitating for the nurseries that would give us access to jobs, the unionisation that would amplify our voice, the equal pay and opportunities that would improve our working lives. The other focussed on women's role as housewives (and to a lesser extent as mothers), calling more simply for money. The first could say it expressed the needs of working-class women, for where pay and conditions were appalling, surely improvement at work was the major concern? The second could equally claim to be the authentic voice of working-class women, for without the qualifications and opportunities that might delude others into 'liberation through jobs', these were the women who were housewives first and wage workers second. And while most feminists came to dissociate themselves from a politics they felt was disruptive, many continued in private to worry about the issue, questioning how far the movement had accommodated itself to this aspect of our lives. When the movement so decisively rejected wages for housework, did this at bottom reflect its middle-class nature – a lack of interest in those who were working at home?

Take this comment from a women who wrote in to WIRES in 1978, distancing herself from the tactics of Wages For Housework, but still identifying with its basic concerns:

> If the women's movement is to be more than just a middle-class movement, we must recognise the reality of most women's lives and stop moralising about whether more money would be 'good for' women or not. Surely what we

want is the choice so that people can make up their minds. Before I had a child the last thing I wanted to be was a housewife. I had this stereotyped image of a typical housewife, her hair in curlers, her exhausted face painted in a pastiche of sexual attractiveness, staggering under armfuls of shopping and screaming kids, doped up to the eyeballs on valium. Uggh! It made me want to run a mile. But now I have a kid of my own, who brings me more pleasure than anything in my life has up to now, I find I am dependent on a man to support me because I have no income of my own. And now I find I have to do his housework as well as my own and the child's, not because he is a male chauvinist pig, bless him, but because in order to support the three of us he has to work 50-60 hours a week at a tiring job, and he doesn't have time for shopping or cooking. Women who tell me £30 a week wages for housework would be bad for my political soul, or that I should stick my kid in a nursery and go and get a job, make me bloody angry.[13]

Having to choose between women as wage workers and women as housewives echoed some of the tensions associated with the New Feminism of the inter-war years, except that this time both sides could claim to be more 'working class'. Dismal as it seems in retrospect, the movement was presented with what seemed an either/or choice, as a confrontation developed that pushed women into opposing, seemingly single-issue, camps. There were repeated efforts towards a more integrated politics, but when it came down to the practice of campaigns, integration proved hard to sustain.

A Woman's Right To Choose

For those concerned to forge links with labour movement politics, the National Abortion Campaign was another focus for action: like the Charter campaign it was prepared to engage in 'mixed' politics; though much more so than in the Charter, the precise role of men was viewed as a problem. Alongside its activities in local groups, in street meetings, in petitions and demonstrations, NAC worked long and hard to secure trade union support, seeing this as a major index of labour movement commitment to women. A motion from the (predominantly female) Tobacco Workers Union at the 1976 Trade Union Congress pledged the labour movement to support abortion rights; two years later a further resolution was passed calling for a national TUC demonstration when necessary to defend the existing Act. In 1979 John Corrie MP put forward a private member's bill that would seriously restrict access to NHS abortions, and the TUC staged its historic and massive march.

For many women in the abortion campaign this was a fantastic breakthrough, though more cynically one could note that supporting state funded abortion costs the labour movement nothing, and indeed that men are much less troubled about the issue than women, for they do not face the guilt and pain of abortion. The day of the demonstration, however, proved contentious, for the TUC arranged a marching order that relegated women's groups to a subsidiary place at the back, a programme of platform speakers that gave space to only one representative from NAC, and male stewards who managed to antagonise many of the women. Much to the discomfiture of union leaders, 'a small group of unruly people' (Len Murray's description) challenged their dominance, forming a breakaway section at the head of the march, and serving as a wonderful diversion for media reports. The ensuing post-mortem hinged partly around the relevance of class: was abortion a woman's issue, a class issue, a combination of the two?

Clearly one argument that swayed male trade unionists (and no doubt many female ones too) was that attacks on our access to abortion hit hardest at working-class women. Abortion on demand could well be presented as a *class* issue, for with restricted rights to an NHS abortion it was surely the poorest who had most to lose? Those with money could always turn to a private clinic; the rest depended on the vagaries of their NHS consultant, and if they lived in the wrong area, they had no choice at all. As Terry Marsland from the Tobacco Workers Union put it, 'Abortion is a women's issue, but it's also a class issue – it affects the whole working class. The people worst affected by any changes in the Act will be the poor, the working class.'[14] Critics of the way the TUC had organised the march homed in on this. The right to abortion facilities, they argued, is about a *woman*'s right to control her own sexuality, not something to be slipped in under the mantle of class politics, as though it only stands scrutiny when you can show how hard conditions are for working-class women and men.[15] Whether women have to scrape together the money for a private abortion or plead with their doctor for one on the NHS, the issue remains the same. Women are being controlled by men, and we will not challenge this if we abandon the campaign to male leadership. The debate was not a simple one of 'women's issue versus class issue', for all involved felt it was primarily the former. But whether you saw abortion as *also* a question of class was sure to affect the place you allotted the unions – and if you saw women themselves as a 'sex class', the whole project was grossly misled.

Radical and revolutionary feminism

These campaigns were only a fraction of what was going on in the 1970s, and I have introduced them mainly to demonstrate difficulties feminists faced where they were trying to link the politics of gender with that of class. But meanwhile a divide had formalised between socialist and radical women: the former preoccupied with the relationship between women's oppression and capitalism (as in the discussion of domestic labour) and between women's autonomous organisation and the labour movement or socialist groups, the latter developing a theory of patriarchy and a much more frontal critique of class politics and of men. In *Sexual Politics* Kate Millet gave a devastating account of the misogyny of male fiction, and argued that patriarchal relations (men dominating women, older men dominating younger) characterised all known societies.[16] In *The Dialectic of Sex* Shulamith Firestone tried to explain this history in terms of male control over women's reproductive capacities. In what today sounds a rather chilling note of liberation through technology, she envisaged a future of 'test tube' babies where the link between sex and reproduction would be broken and women could finally free themselves from their slavish dependence on men.[17] From this angle, male power over women had its own separate history: it was not a reflection of class power but an entire system of dominance in its own right.

Most of this early writing came from America; in Britain it fed into arguments about the political autonomy of the women's movement, the exclusion of men from meetings and demonstrations, and the nature and sources of women's oppression. It is hard to imagine from the standpoint of the eighties, but men were not explicitly excluded from national conference until their disruptive interventions at the 1971 National Women's Liberation Conference played them out; the central office of the London Women's Liberation Workshop was not closed to men till 1974. Radical feminists took the lead in arguing for exclusion, and indeed in creating a lifestyle of women who lived without men. As one recalled in 1979,

> Political independence and personal separatism ... raised the issue of lifestyle politics. Radical feminists were for it all the way: we wanted to leave men no matter what, we started squatting so we could live with other women, we acquired of necessity new 'male' skills of plumbing, electricity, carpentry and car maintenance, setting up our own discos and then forming bands to dance to. We cut our hair very short and stopped wearing 'women's' clothes, we stopped smiling and being 'nice'. We went over the top in fact.[18]

By the later seventies a new voice of revolutionary feminism had joined the fray. In an influential paper on 'The Need For Revolutionary Feminism' that was first discussed in a workshop at the 1977 annual conference, Sheila Jeffreys launched her attack, not initially against socialist feminism, but against what she feared was a liberal take-over of the women's liberation movement.[19] Arguing that 'life-stylism' was substituting for the tasks of wresting power from men, and that a self-appointed role as 'educators' was leading some groups of women to play down their anger in order to make their ideas more appealing to wider constituencies, she identified women as a 'sex-class', united in their oppression by men.

> As a revolutionary feminist, I see in existence two class systems, one is the economic class system based on the relationship of people to production, the second is the sex-class system, based on the relationship of people to reproduction. As a woman, it is the second class system which oppresses me most and which dominates and pollutes my day-to-day existence, through my fear on the streets at night, the eyes, the gestures and comments of males in every contact with them, etc. To be a socialist feminist, I would have to accept a unity of interests between myself and a group of men and to accept that my fears and humiliations came from capitalism and not men, and that I cannot do.[20]

More centred on issues of power than what they felt was the broader and therefore vaguer spectrum of radical feminism, compatible in principle with socialism (because of the notion of an economic class system) but definitively *not* with the practice of working with men, revolutionary feminism came to focus on issues of rape and domestic violence as the key areas for action.

> Our strategy should be to build the *class* consciousness of women. Our tactics must be those that expose male power and how it operates. We suggest actions around rape and violence within the family including incest will have the most consciousness raising power among women.[21]

The issues of rape and domestic violence were of course already among the questions taken up by the women's movement. The first refuge for battered women had been set up by Erin Pizzey in London in 1972, and by the mid-70s there were many more in existence, funded by government or charities, but organised by the women involved. From 1975, when Erin Pizzey stormed out of its second national conference, the Women's Aid Federation developed as an explicitly feminist organisation for women who worked in and around refuges, and a major women's movement activity.[22] The first Rape Crisis Centre was set up in London in 1976, and this too was soon to be joined by more. Revolutionary feminism now offered a theoretical basis for such work and to the campaign that developed subsequently: Women Against Violence Against Women.

It is an interesting comment on the continuing legacy of socialist language that revolutionary feminism should have talked of 'raising (sex) class consciousness', and indeed that its analysis still acknowledged the exploitative relations of the *economic* class system. But this was not to imply space for more traditional class concerns, for as Sheila Jeffreys noted, when women and men are locked into the bitter struggles of the 'sex class system', there is no room for joint action as workers. And while at one level there might have been no reason why revolutionary feminists should not work on a variety of fronts – taking up issues of rape and domestic violence, but also continuing the more traditional work around nurseries, employment, abortion, and so on – in practice women tended to separate out into these different activities, depending on their theoretical concerns. At a conference in Edinburgh in 1977, radical and revolutionary feminists were still discussing whether to concentrate their energies on rape and physical violence, or to fight male power on all of its fronts, including relationships, abortions, workplaces, schools, nurseries, and so on; but as a participant reported in WIRES, 'some women seemed to think that spreading ourselves too wide .was the cause of the liberal takeover'.[23] For revolutionary feminism the keynote was to be rejection of men, with campaigns against male sexuality, and then by extension against all heterosexuality assuming the definitive role. In 1979 the Leeds Revolutionary Feminists sprung another bombshell with their paper 'Political Lesbianism: The Case Against Heterosexuality'.[24] Heterosexual sex was collaboration with the enemy: men were not just poor allies on a march; they were the enemy itself in your bed.

Class on the run

By this time, in fact, class was being put more firmly on the defensive, by socialist and radical/revolutionary alike. The growth of Women's Aid refuges and Rape Crisis Centres had brought the real violence in men's relations with women out into the open, confirming much of what radical feminists had always argued about male domination, and giving weight to the revolutionary feminist line. 'Reclaim the night' marches through London's Soho and other sex-shop areas built on earlier campaigns against the degradation of women, but with slogans like 'pornography is the theory and rape is the practice', they had a much sharper edge. Sexuality had been a major preoccupation within the Women's Liberation Movement from its inception, but in the first years it was transforming the troubled course of heterosexual relations that tended to focus debate. Lesbian feminists had questioned this emphasis, but rarely from a separatist stance; involved as many of them had been with the simultaneous growth of Gay Liberation, they were used to working with men. But by the second half of the seventies lesbianism was more frequently (though never exclusively) associated with political separatism; while heterosexuality was exposed to harsher review.

As the climate of opinion altered so too did the demands of the Women's Liberation Movement. The first four had all hovered in some way around questions of money and work. Equal pay, equal education and opportunities, twenty-four hour nurseries, free contraception and abortion on demand: all were amenable to some kind of class perspective for on every issue it seemed that *working-class* women bore the brunt. They were the ones whose pay lagged furthest behind the men's. They were the ones who lost out most in our 'free' but by no means equal system of public education, and found themselves in the dead-end jobs. They could never afford nannies or private nurseries; they had no alternatives to the NHS.

I am not suggesting that the movement formulated these demands as relevant to working-class women alone – as already noted, it was part of the confidence of those early years that we could see oppression attacking *every* woman's life. But as far as inserting them into conventional class politics was concerned, there were obvious points of entry. They drew attention to the super-exploitation of women in low-paid jobs, to the appalling public provision for nursery schools, to the unfair distribution of family planning clinics and the inequities of an abortion law that made abortion legal, but free only if your doctor approved. We argued for them as demands for women, *all* women, but if we were prepared to bend our principles a bit, we could also make a powerful case in terms that any labour movement activist should be able to accept (they didn't necessarily, but that's another story!).

Later developments shifted this emphasis. The 1974 conference in Edinburgh added the fifth demand for legal and financial independence and the sixth demand for an end to discrimination against lesbians and a right to our own self-defined sexuality. Legal and financial independence may sound an ambiguous one, in some ways more typically like the demand of a middle-class movement, for short of massive increases in female wages and huge improvements in child care provision, what meaning can it have to a working-class wife? But it was part and parcel of a growing attack on marriage and its structures of dependence: on the way, for example, that taxation and social security practices acted as if men were the breadwinners and women the dependants, or the way that unions still negotiated 'family wages' for men and peanuts for women. Asserting as it did a woman's right to be independent of a man, the fifth demand cut across much of what had been taken for granted in labour movement politics.

And then an end to discrimination against lesbians and a right to a self-defined sexuality: a demand that really did put the cat among the pigeons, seeming to confirm all the *other* media images of feminists – not just a bunch of middle-class moaners, but man-hating lesbians as well. Earlier attempts to discuss lesbianism had met with considerable resistance, most actively from some of the women in socialist groups but passively too from others. And class again had been one of the underlying themes. If feminism became publicly identified with lesbianism, how would this affect the attitude of the 'ordinary woman' to the women's movement? (ordinary women are always assumed to be heterosexual). Or if the right to a self-defined sexuality became one of the key demands, how would this strike those pursuing more 'serious' economic concerns?

Such reservations never entirely disappeared. But by the second half of the seventies the majority of those attending women's movement conferences were assuming a more confident stance, insisting that the critique of heterosexuality and/or male violence should be taken as pre-eminent concerns. In 1978 a huge and explosive national conference in Birmingham (the last of its kind, for no one has since volunteered to stage such another!) finally agreed the seventh demand: 'freedom from intimidation by the threat or use of violence or sexual coercion, regardless of marital status. An end to the laws, assumptions and institutions that perpetuate male dominance and men's aggression towards women'. At the same time the right to a self-defined sexuality was extricated from its sixth place on the list and highlighted as the preamble to all other demands. In a period of considerable heat and tension, women were rejecting the language and politics of class, declaring a vision that had sexuality at its core. The troubled and troubling atmosphere of the time is neatly captured in a recipe by 'Ever Wilde':

> Take a few revolutionary feminists, a few socialist feminists, add a pinch of liberalism and a sprinkling of fanaticism, one dozen seven syllabled words, a pint of plenary and two microphones, mix them all together to produce the most boring headache causing, thirst creating, women hating, classist, racist, ageist conference discussion mind boggling couple of hours any woman could possibly have to suffer in the cause of feminism.[25]

Yet even as these tensions threatened to divide feminists for ever, there was a process of convergence, for the lessons of radical feminism were hitting home and the language of patriarchy and male domination was entering socialist vocabulary as well. For women still active in trade union or socialist politics, these were times of reassessment; socialism was being forced to bow to feminism instead of the other way round. In 1979 Sheila

Rowbotham, Lynne Segal and Hilary Wainwright brought out *Beyond the Fragments: Feminism and the Making of Socialism*, which drew on the experience of the women's movement to construct a devastating critique of the kind of Leninist politics that still informed the practice of so many socialist groups.[26] With its scorching analysis of the socialist 'experts', intervening with their 'correct line' to 'raise' political consciousness, it coincided with a rare moment of socialist self-consciousness; we can hardly hear the language now without an internal shudder.

Socialists in the left groups were under attack, and socialists in the Labour Party came in for their share too. The most radical edge of Labour Party policy in the seventies seemed its alternative economic strategy: a programme for revival that depended on a major shift from private to public control; nationalisation of top industries; planning agreements to subordinate the others; controls on the movement of capital; planned trade; industrial democracy; planning on a scale unknown in peace-time Britain. But as feminists now pointed out, it was a strategy that made few if any concessions to women. Full employment was discussed with minimal reference to the growing army of part-time women workers; the decline of manufacturing industry was prioritised as the fundamental problem, and nobody seemed to notice that this was where men rather than women worked; growth was projected as the key issue without any attempt at eliminating inequality.[27] Here as elsewhere, the problems of workers were being discussed as if workers by definition are men. If class politics wanted to prove its relevance to women, it would have to do a great deal better.

Socialist feminism was going on the offensive, attacking the ways that unions organised (men controlling union executives), the kind of constituency they typically represented (white, male, skilled workers), and the sorts of bargains they usually struck (high wages for the men, not much left over for the women). Partly in response to the Working Women's Charter, the TUC had agreed a package of demands relating to wages, training, nurseries, abortion, maternity leave, and so on. But successes here proved mostly paper gains. The TUC adopted exemplary charters for women at work, for under-fives provision, for positive action inside the unions themselves. Yet since the late seventies women have slid further down the wages table, been concentrated more and more into part-time jobs, and when redundancy hits their firm, very often been the first to go. The most determinedly socialist of socialist feminists was beginning to lose her cool.

As far as union practices are concerned, feminists began to hit at some of the most cherished traditions of the labour movement. The family wage was again an issue. Criticism mounted over the ways that unions still claimed a higher wage for men as breadwinners, condoning much lower ones for women as dependants, and this practice was identified as one of the key obstacles to genuinely equal pay.[28] The sexual segregation of the labour force, which keeps men in better paid skilled jobs and women in the worst paid unskilled ones was attacked. More and more women came to view this segregation as reflecting not so much the capitalist organisation of work, nor even the ways that women have been deprived of training opportunities, but at a certain level, naked male power.[29] The principle of free collective bargaining was denounced as a survival-of-the-fittest hangover and one still subservient to that 'sacred cow' of differentials. Some even suggested that government incomes policies (anathema by the late seventies to any self-respecting trade unionist) were the better deal for women, an issue that sparked considerable debate.[30] On an escalating range of issues, feminists were attacking the bastions of class politics, and when in 1984 Beatrix Campbell described the labour movement as the 'men's movement',[31] she was giving voice to what had become the position not just of radical or revolutionary feminists but of many socialist feminists as well.

Women in unions and Labour Party

Since 1978 there has been no national women's movement conference, and arguments between feminists have been anguished and acute. This coincided, however, with an extended period of right-wing government which was to be partially contested by the election of left-wing councils. Many women have subsequently turned their energies to campaigns within the labour movement: joining or re-joining the Labour Party; becoming more active within their unions; taking on jobs with the new women's committees or equal opportunities committees that have been a novel feature of local council work (at least in London) through the 1980s. This was not just a return to pre-feminist thought, for such women took with them that sharper sense of male domination they had developed in the previous decade – and they have felt themselves intensely up against the men.

But they have also of course been up against some women, for while many in the labour movement will see 'men's movement' as no more than fact, for others it is a less telling description. Implying as it does that decades of campaigning work have made no significant incursions into trade union or Labour Party practice, it can be much resented by those who were around in those earlier years. And coinciding as it has with a period of political crisis, it can put us cruelly on the spot. Few women active in today's labour movement will deny the presence of male power, but with the horrifying spectre of another five years of Tory misrule, the 1980s dawned as a decade of pessimism and retreat. Should women's voices then swell the choir of condemnation when the unions themselves were in disarray and the Labour Party seemed in such terminal crisis? Could we really afford to focus on conflicts of gender when all around us swept the issues of class? What, in this context, should the women do?

Many feminists in the unions and Labour Party chose to take the offensive, arguing that the very weakness of these bodies reflected their denial of women, and that unless equality was placed firmly on the agenda the process of decline would continue. Over the past ten years the voices of self-conscious feminism have spoken with increasing confidence inside both unions and Labour Party, as women's committees have proliferated within most of the major unions, women's sections been set up or revitalised by more and more constituency parties, women's committees been established by a number of Labour councils. New forums have been created and old ones brought back into play. Attendance at the National Conference of Labour Women has risen to 650 and attendance at the TUC Women's Conference to over 300; the former is increasingly marked by its feminist concerns, while in the latter, as one observer put it, feminism runs 'like a thin, frayed but live wire through the proceedings'.[32]

That the work of local council women's committees or equal opportunities committees should reflect the concerns of feminism comes as no surprise: it was the women's movement that precipitated their existence. But at the women's conferences of both TUC and Labour Party, the range of motions also reflects what have been thought of as women's movement concerns. Resolutions have called for action against sexual harassment at work or the portrayal of women in the media; called on local authorities to fund refuges for battered women and their children; expressed heart-felt support for the women at Greenham Common; condemned discrimination against lesbians and gay men. The 1981 TUC Women's Conference called on the General Council to launch a campaign to raise the consciousness of male trade unionists about taking an equal part in housework and childcare; in 1982 a motion was passed that criticised the masculine focus of the alternative economic strategy. The language might not be that of women's liberation conferences, but even here the impact is felt: by 1984 the 'chairman' of the TUC Women's Conference had submitted to the ignominious title of chair; while those once welcomed as fraternal delegates are nowadays greeted as 'sororal'. In both form and content the link is there. Few motions to do with women are ruled out of court, and the majority have won support.

Conflicts, however, remain and they have centred primarily on what institutional powers the women should claim. Within both unions and Labour Party, the women's conference has had a purely advisory role, with the status of the National Conference of Labour Women so hazy that its proceedings are not even officially minuted! Though the TUC General Council and the Labour Party National Executive Committee both have seats reserved for women, those who fill them are elected by the (largely male) annual gatherings, and not by the conferences of women. The Women's Advisory Committee (WAC) that in the case of the unions runs women's affairs through the intervening year, has a majority of its members selected from the General Council: even in 1984, after reforms to increase women's representation, WAC was made up of sixteen members from the General Council (ten men and six women) and only ten chosen by the conference. The parallel Labour Women's Advisory Committee is composed of two women from each of the regions; once again it is not the women's conference that determines its composition. And in both unions and party, the far-reaching resolutions passed by the women's conferences rarely get much further; 'women's motions' at the TUC or Labour Party Conference are debated in half-empty halls and when they are contentious, they are usually voted down. The notable and most recent exception is that the annual Labour Party Conference has finally passed a resolution in defence of lesbian and gay rights; a small cynical voice may once again note that this is not something that costs much money.

Not surprisingly then, the striking edge of feminism within both these contexts has been its insistence that the women should claim more power. Successive motions at the TUC Women's Conference have called for greater representation of women on WAC and more women's seats on the General Council; for an automatic place on the agenda of the annual TUC Congress for some of the resolutions passed at the women's conference; for the rotation of the position of chair of the WAC and women's conference (a move aimed largely at the commanding presence of Marie Patterson, who for sixteen years monopolised these positions); and for the formation of a Conference Arrangements Committee – directly elected by the conference – which would then by-pass some of the work of WAC. But with a few notable exceptions (the conference carried in 1977 a resolution calling for the doubling of their representatives on WAC and for seven extra seats for women on the General Council) these motions have been lost. Delegates may be united by their commitment to women, but they do not agree on ways of achieving their goal.

Within the Labour Party things have moved much faster. Women have organised primarily through the women's sections, bodies that once declined into a supportive, fund-raising role, but have been radically revitalised since. One of the avenues for change here has been the Women's Action Campaign (another WAC!), set up as an offshoot of the Campaign for Labour Party Democracy in 1980; the demands it currently organises around relate exclusively to institutional reform. The women's conference should be strengthened in power. It should have the right to send five resolutions to the annual party conference which would then be automatically included on the agenda; the right to elect its own Women's Advisory Committee; the right to elect the five women who fill the women's seats on the party's national executive. There should be a rules conference to reconsider party proceedings and practices; there should be at least one woman on the shortlist when councillors and MPs are selected. Not, it might seem, the most earth-shattering and revolutionary of demands, yet as one of the activists in WAC has put it, 'it is possible to win support for quite lengthy and elaborate resolutions on women's rights, i.e. abortion, childcare facilities, even support for more controversial questions such as what attitude to take towards rape victims ... But we cannot get much support for democracy for women.'[33] In contrast to the TUC women, Labour Party women *have* approved far-reaching proposals on party organisation in their conferences, but year after year fail to secure passage through the masculine barriers of the full party affair. In both the unions and the party the pattern it seems is the same: as long as the 'women's motions' appear as additions to general concerns they can go as far as they like; once they edge into the overall balance of power, once they imply reforms that might make these motions reality, their presumption is rapidly squashed.

Disagreement distorted by class?

Opponents of institutional reform have expressed impatience with its concerns – and it is an argument for which I have some sneaking sympathy: it does seem unfortunate that feminist energies within both unions and Labour Party should be swallowed up in organisational affairs. Yet unless women gain a more powerful platform their whispers will go unheeded, and though it would be a sorry conclusion if institutional reform took precedence over policy, we should not have to choose between these two. The associated difficulty is that the focus on female representation has been identified as a retreat from the class: thus even David Blunkett, leader of Sheffield council, has talked of 'not wanting the women's movement to sap the energy of the class struggle' and has defended Sheffield's refusal to create specifically women's committees partly along these lines.[34]

The implication – and often enough the explicit complaint – is that it is middle-class women who pursue the issues of institutional control and that 'real' working women have more sense than to follow. The feminists have been identified as those from white collar jobs; their pre-occupations are seen as an import from outside. And of course within the labour movement, more so than anywhere, to be middle class is to be discredited; reveal yourself as 'trendy' and you are on the way out. The Labour Party may celebrate the unity of 'workers by hand or by brain' but in practice it is uneasy with this; the TUC may accommodate both manual and non-manual workers within its structures, but this does not dissolve the tensions. With the hierarchically structured labour force that characterises contemporary capitalism, differences between white collar and manual, 'middle' class and 'working' class, are inevitably among the forces at play, and feminist intervention has been dogged by this.

The equation of feminists with outsiders from the middle class has a particularly strong appeal within the labour movement, and the history of women's trade unionism has been punctuated by this complaint. To return briefly to an earlier moment, the role for a separate Women's Trade Union League and for its sister organisation, the National Federation of Women Workers (NFWW), came under question in the early twentieth century, partly because of the trebling in women's trade union membership during the First World War which brought those who had worked their way up through their own unions more to the fore. 'Women members who had risen to official posts in their "mixed" unions therefore felt confident that they no longer required the help of middle-class women "outsiders".'[35] In the restructuring of the TUC after the war, separate organisation for women tended to be associated precisely with these outsiders.

With commendable humility – though perhaps with hindsight to unfortunate ends – the middle-class feminists bowed out. In 1920 the TUC set up its General Council, with representation from seventeen industrial groups; after a successful amendment moved by the NFWW this was extended to include the two seats for women representing women workers. A Women Workers Group was set up as a sub-committee of the General Council and the Women's Trade Union League agreed to dissolve itself, holding its final meeting in 1921. Because of new TUC rules which excluded non-trade unionists from election, its most active surviving members (Mary Macarthur died in 1921) had no place on this Women Workers Group. The merely advisory TUC Women's Conference was subsequently established in 1925. The separate women's union had meantime dissolved itself, voting in 1920 to merge with the National Union of General Workers which by 1930 was sending no women representatives to the TUC! A parallel process of absorption was at work in the Labour Party: the Women's Labour League was reformed in 1918 as the women's section of the Labour Party; women were allotted their seats on the party's national executive, but these were to be filled, as we know, by votes from the largely male annual conference.

When the issue of 'separatism' came up again in the 1970s, it emerged in sharp debates at the TUC Women's Conference over whether it should remain in existence. Congress itself had suggested that a specifically women's organisation was now anomalous, and year after year motions at the women's conference proposed its abolition. The arguments were as might be predicted: those calling for an end maintained that a separate conference for women workers only hived off issues that should be taken up by the movement as a whole; those opposed to abolition pointed out that without their conference the women would have nothing.

What was less predictable was the line-up on either side, for at this point the axis of debate was twofold, and it was not the 'middle-class feminists' who defended their separate sphere. On the one hand was complacency versus impatience. The old guard in the General Council and WAC tended to support the status quo, defending the women's conference by its record of achievements and arguing that it must remain. Ranged against them were eager new activists – sometimes from unions who had only recently sent their first delegations – who felt the conference was little better than a talking shop: a 'well-intentioned but meaningless concept'.[36] Along this axis, the more radical proposal looked like abolition: if the women were to make their mark, it must be in the mainstream of the TUC. But along another axis was the issue of separatism versus amalgamation, a question the women's movement had long made its own. Do women need their own organisations as the basis for their strength, or should they compete on so-called equal terms with men? On the question of the future of the women's conference, it seemed that 'feminist' arguments could be employed with equal coherence to either conclusion: one of the ironies of the debate was that it had Len Murray and the General Council defending the 'separatist' position!

The complexities defied simple labels, but labels were still applied. It became commonplace through the 1970s to characterise the supporters of abolition as better-off women from white collar jobs, those who thought equality was just round the corner, or as one delegate from the shop-workers' union put it, those 'bright young women libs saying that we could do away with it'.[37] When the General Council produced a report on trade union structure and development in 1972, it commented that the moves to abolish the women's conference had come mainly from non-manual public sector unions where women had supposedly achieved a greater degree of equality with men, and therefore considered the conference irrelevant.[38] When NALGO moved the abolition of the conference in 1973, a speaker against suggested it was union inexperience that provoked this move: 'I want to remind NALGO that it is only a few years ago that they affiliated to the TUC. I am sure the young lady who ably moved the motion will have a change of heart once she gets accustomed to seeing the way the thing works.'[39] And when the issue was most recently debated, a representative from the Women's Advisory Committee made a similar comment: 'I think it is significant that the motion is proposed by those relatively privileged sisters who come from the fields of employment where equal pay and better opportunities for women do exist.'[40]

The comment was a gross distortion of the spirit of this and the previous motions, for misguided as I think they were, they in no way implied that women's battles were won. But throughout the debates the divide between manual and non-manual workers was one of the forces in play, and what were complex tactical issues got shoved into the categories of class. The truth of the matter is that it *was* white collar unions – NALGO, NUJ, the Association of Broadcasting and Allied Staffs – that in the 1970s most consistently supported abolition, but then many white collar unions also voted against. Class was not the determinant of political position, but class reductionism fed on the arguments, breeding mutual distrust.

In the 1980s the arguments have shifted: all concerned agree that the conference should remain. The face of 'middle-class feminism' is now seen in the moves to extend its power. And indeed it *has* been those from white collar unions who have most consistently pushed this position, and while it was the Tobacco Workers Union that made the running over the question of abortion, on many other issues white collar women took the lead. Commenting on proposals at the 1983 conference to make some of the women's motions mandatory on the agenda of the TUC conference, Kate Holman from the NUJ observed that divisions between white collar and blue collar were still a problem:

> Originally the proposals came from smaller white-collar unions such as ACTT, BIFU and the National Union of Journalists, all of whom have a reputation for being radical at conference. Sadly a rift has developed between these 'radical' white-collar unions and the 'traditional' blue-collar unions.
>
> Women in the public sector and manufacturing industries, suffering the most vicious effects of low pay, redundancies, lack of childcare and other basic services, and then bearing the brunt of domestic responsibilities on top of their paid work, may be justified in regarding debates about what motion goes where as a bit of a luxury. But good policies by

themselves will not bring change.[41]

In the case of the Labour Party, the women's conference has drawn overwhelmingly on delegates from constituency parties – few are sent by their unions – and critics of the party will be quick to tell you that constituency activists are not the working class. Opponents of the Women's Action Campaign regard it as both middle class and London-based (the latter itself a code word for middle-class trendies), and while it has won substantial support from constituency activists, its politics are viewed with some suspicion by leading women trade unionists. Rightly or wrongly, the public face of labour movement feminism is as women from middle-class jobs, an equation that has *some* basis in sociological fact, but does scant justice to the many women in manual employment whose commitment to equality is as fervent as anyone could desire.

The way that class enters into the scenario is complex, for women in manual trades have had if anything the more shattering experiences of male power: more of them are likely to work part time, and as such will have faced a long history of union disinterest in their problems; more of them need upgrading to get 'equal pay' (this was the issue for the women at Ford's) and unions have been predictably slow to act on this issue. But women are having to forge their unity in a context that is partly defined by class, and this sets them difficult questions. Die-hards in the labour movement still use the proclaimed primacy of class to dismiss as irrelevant the under-representation of women; feminists in the labour movement have often responded with what seems like a mirror assertion of the primacy of gender. A vicious circle gets going that limits our options, for while most women are in practice tussling with issues of both gender *and* class – and many with race as well – that either/or dichotomy blocks our way out. The picture is not as bleak as this sounds, for women *are* transforming the labour movement, and the dynamism of women's trade unionism is there for all to see.[42] But the path of feminism inside the unions and Labour Party is still a troubled one – and the conflicts are not only with men.

'Classism': the enemy within

Meanwhile class was smouldering away along another fuse to explode into those questions of privilege inside the women's movement. The 1977 National Women's Liberation conference saw the first workshop on revolutionary feminism, but it also saw a workshop on 'classism', in which working-class and middle-class women tried to face out the tensions between them. In 1978 a Working Class Women's Liberation Newsletter was launched, and it was full of long-repressed anger against the patronage of middle-class women. The arguments here cut across the revolutionary and socialist feminist divide, as Chris Joyce made clear in 1979:

> Over the last few years I have come to realise that not only is the Women's Liberation Movement made up of middle-class women but that many of these women have the same misconceptions and prejudices about working-class women as straight middle-class society has about the working class in general ... These assumptions are apparent in all areas of the Women's Liberation Movement from the revolutionary feminists who insist that all women are equally oppressed and refuse to admit that working-class women are oppressed by their middle-class attitudes, to socialist feminists who cry 'we must get more working-class women into the movement' yet refuse to acknowledge those of us who are already here.[43]

The very guilt of the movement about its relationship to working-class women 'out there' had fostered the assumption that feminists were all middle class: as one woman wrote in WIRES in 1976, 'that the Women's Liberation Movement is middle class is a cliché, especially if you are middle class. Otherwise it's an oppression.'[44] When working-class women questioned the cliché, they were told they had mistaken their class.

> As to those of us who do dare to criticise there are lots of ways of answering, including denying a woman's right to call herself working class because of some magical event in her life which wiped out all her previous experience at one stage or because of some behaviour which she displays not commonly associated with being common. 'You're not working class, you've been to university/dropped out of university/didn't get to university but you're here anyway/-your parents go abroad for their holidays/your dad owns his house/you're in the women's movement/you live with middle-class women/you don't wipe your nose on the teatowel or have newspaper in the toilet/etc. etc.' If all that

doesn't work they'll smile at you with glazed eyes and pat you on the head or pretend they didn't understand what you said, could you explain again (this is a good one – very confusing on the fiftieth try) or they'll just pretend they heard what they wanted to hear and leave you believing you actually got through. Very upsetting when you eventually realise you didn't.[45]

In Evelyn Tension's influential *You don't need a degree to read the writing on the wall* the argument was partly (and revealingly) directed against a student culture that scorned consumerism, rejected security, and glorified poverty – easy enough, as she says, if you have 'a degree, a bank balance and a family to fall back on. And no children.'[46] Feminism had, as she indicated, created its own lifestyle, a culture in which you felt you had to apologise if you wore a skirt to a women's group meeting, in which communal living earnt you more points than nuclear families, in which keeping a spotless house made you look like a victim of feminine guilt. The fashion was never universal, and from quite early on feminists were noting the predilection for short hair and trousers and bemoaning the absence of feminists with 'style'. But even this could sound like the private joke of a little sub-culture, revelling in its difference even when it seemed to say the opposite.

For virtually all involved in the movement there was a clash of cultures between their way of life as feminists and the families they had come from, but for middle-class women this could seem more unambiguously a strength. 'Free of the draggy orthodox middle classes but still able to take advantage of certain privileges, securities, connections. And an alternative society – the movement – for comfort, fun, support and self-expression.'[47] For working-class women it was much more difficult and many felt torn between loyalties to their friends in the movement and loyalties to their family and home. Tasha, a working-class feminist, described these tensions in heart-felt terms in an interview for *Spare Rib* in 1977.

I brought some friends back to see my father and I felt that they were putting him down. He may be a man, but he's my father, and he's working class and I feel that they've had far more chances in life than he's ever had. That's something that's really important about class: the chances, the choices, expectations and mobility, being able to have the space that everyone's always talking about. Space to do things – my father's never had fucking space, manoeuvreability. He's never been able to choose between this and that or that. I feel incredibly split when I'm with middle-class feminists and my father's there, 'cos I know that I feel far more empathy with him than for her, my sister.[48]

The problem identified by working-class feminists was not just insensitivity to such dilemmas, it was also a question of power. Classism, as Marlene Packwood has described it in a more recent contribution, is

a specific oppression where the rules, values, mores and ideals of one class are imposed upon another, within the hierarchy of class values. Within feminism it filters through from middle-class to working-class women, denying them a language, banning them from self-expression, labelling them ignorant, stupid, coarse, bombastic, rough, uneducated, ineffectual.[49]

It was not just that some women had more than others – though this was felt as bad enough. It was also that they could employ their privileges to determine the terms of debate.

Since the late seventies the accusations have mounted; 'classism' has become a feminist term. The very ageing of the movement has been partly the cause, for activists now have more varieties of power, and differences of income are more marked than before. When some women speak from the securities of their better paid job, and others from the dole queue and the pittance of SS, it is harder to talk of their common oppression: their experiences too obviously diverge. If the former also have greater access to publishing and the media, their advantages can serve to dominate and control, for theirs is then the public face and they can define the issues. The success of feminism within certain contexts has heightened the problem, for as well as the extraordinary achievements of feminist publishing and feminist presses, as well as the increased opportunities for women in academic institutions to teach courses on women (making a living, as critics would put it, out of the ideas and passions of the movement), as well as all this, feminism has become a growth area inside the local state.

In 1981 the Labour Party won control of the Greater London Council; even more significantly, it won control with a new wave of radical councillors who elected Ken Livingstone as their leader. Partly through the impact of the women's movement at large, partly through the activities of women inside the Labour Party, and partly through the influence of Livingstone himself, the new administration was more open than usual to the ideas of feminism. What gave this substance was ironically the Law Lords' decision to reverse the major policy on which the GLC had been elected: cheap bus and tube fares. In 1981 five Law Lords ruled that the GLC had acted illegally in cutting fares by 25 per cent and cancelled the supplementary rate that had been levied to pay for the policy; the Council was subsequently landed with a bill for £125 million to cover the resulting deficit. GLC rates were doubled in 1982 to pay off this money, but disastrous as this was at the time, it had its silver lining. 'The GLC budget would be raised in one leap on to a plateau which could otherwise only have been reached after a long, painful and unpopular climb.'[50] Once the deficit was paid off, the higher rate could then finance other activities, and in 1983 there was an unprecedented sevenfold expansion in the programme of the newly created women's committee – up to seven million pounds. Not a lot of money spread out over all the women in the Greater London area, but from virtually nil funding an amazing leap.

As this and parallel developments in other councils (the first women's committee was not in the GLC but the London Borough of Lewisham) created more chances for women, issues of race and class were brought to the surface. However tiny the budgets they controlled, those involved were having to decide who to employ and what to support: would they use their new-found if limited powers to reproduce a 'middle-class clique'; would they service the activities of black and working-class women? And if the latter, would it be charity extended by middle-class 'sisters' or real power passed on to working-class and black women? The voices of black and working-class women have helped settle the question more in their favour, though no one engaged in the new 'politics of funding' can be complacent with the results: when women's groups are set in competition for their tiny slice of a cake the tensions can be frequent and quelling. The one thing that *has* unequivocally emerged – in these and the wider debates – is that 'sisterhood' is not enough of a guide, and the cautious optimism of three working-class feminists in 1985 expresses both the anxieties and the hopes of our time:

For the moment we feel that the women's movement is in a state of change, with the realisation that being women together is not enough and that the differences between us have to be taken account of. The divisions in the women's movement have knocked our confidence, but we believe that the end of the pretence that we are all white, middle class, thin, able bodied, childless and from a christian background (or that if we're not we at least wish we were) is a positive thing. The women's movement can (and must) change to take account of the ways we oppress each other as well as the ways in which we are oppressed.[51]

Sisters fall out

The issue of classism is not of course peculiar to the women's movement: as an obstacle to joint endeavours it can work wherever those from different class backgrounds are engaged on a common concern. It operates in trade unions that draw their members from a variety of occupations; in Labour Party meetings that bring together both working-class and middle-class activists; in parent-teachers' associations; in any of a variety of campaigns. Through all these we may note the exclusivity of those who share a common intellectual or cultural heritage, the tendency for those with middle-class jobs to set the terms of debate and dominate positions of influence, the recurrent patterns of patronage and apology and guilt. In all these the fact that some have an intimate experience of poverty while others know it only second-hand sets up barriers: the latter may alternate between a heady romanticism and an absent-minded acceptance of what is their own relative freedom. Accused of ignorance of working-class life they may well fall back on the 'trick' noted by working-class feminists, finding 'a long lost working-class relative who is produced like a rabbit out of a hat'[52] and who proves that they are not middle class at all. (I know this trick well; I have employed it myself.)

What gives class such intensity within women's politics is that we are all supposed to be sisters, and when we fall out we do it with a vengeance. The very 'life-stylism' of the women's movement is partly the problem, for if it expresses a desire for homogeneity it also implies an intolerance of difference. Compared with the relatively anonymous meetings of unions or political parties, women's groups convey an atmosphere of intimate engagement –

and there must be few in or on the margins of the women's movement who have never felt left out in the cold. The strength of sisterhood is also its weakness: it's great if you belong, it's terrible if you don't.

Yet in their critique of this, working-class feminists have not so much overturned sisterhood as demanded that it be made more substantial. Marlene Packwood, for example, has argued for income-sharing as the precondition for change: 'Time has come for a long overdue discussion and implementation of income-sharing.'[53] Imagine someone proposing this in a Labour Party ward: you might get support for a motion on national policies of income redistribution, but you would meet a wall of disbelief if you suggested that ward members should share out their incomes. I make the contrast not to pour scorn on the idea of income sharing within the women's movement but to highlight the continuing power of sisterhood and its vision. There is a greater expectation of unity than we might find in other areas of political life, and when, as so often, feminists fall short they are exposed to greater attack.

One of the members of the first group to produce WIRES commented recently on the difference between the way she perceived the problem of class and what she felt to be the dominant mood today:

> Like the class thing: I remember reading *You don't need a degree to read the writing on the wall* when I was at WIRES, and I loved it, and I thought, this is absolutely fantastic. There wasn't an understanding of class then, and as a working-class woman, I had to struggle along with that. I remember in the Chapeltown [Leeds] women's group when I said I wanted to talk about class one woman telling me what class was about, and me feeling I'm sure it's important, but I had no means with which to say why it was important. But for me, though the women's group was predominantly middle class, if we add up who's who, it wasn't *all* middle class. The other things compensated; even if I was in a middle-class setting, with middle-class assumptions and all that, which I was struggling against, compared to the rest of my life it was a real treat! The anti-thing, of having other women be your enemy, other women represent a power over you, that just felt really alien – I'd hate it, if I was ... So although the working-class thing was starting, and I could understand it, I

couldn't really relate to it as a lot of women seemed to be doing, and being very angry with their sisters. And I used to put it down to London again ... It was if the London women were down a hole and were dragging all the rest of us down with them, and I didn't want to go – I wanted the place where I was learning to grow. That's why I stayed being a part of the movement, because I was finally getting to do things with my life, and that's what for me, feminism was about.[54]

She stayed part of the movement; others have become more distanced. In the confidence of the late 1960s and early 1970s, you did not have to be the most oppressed, for it was enough to be a woman. Now that the cloak of sisterhood has been drawn aside, revealing more starkly the multiple differences in the experiences and chances of women; now that feminism has become part respectable, opening up career paths for some, yet bringing few improvements for others; now that fifteen years of the contemporary women's movement has run its course, making major incursions in our social norms but hardly budging the grim statistics; now where are we? Because sisterhood did not solve our problems – and in retrospect it could not have done so – we are inclined to turn on each other. The anger unleashed can be deeply depressing.

Today's arguments over classism strike chords in that old song about feminism being bourgeois, but the melody is far from the same. With the major exception of the debates around abortion (where the issue of class *has* raised questions about the scope of the campaign's demands), class is not really being used to question our concerns. The arguments are not about how class myopia may have limited the movement's demands, nor indeed about the very real tensions experienced by women who are involved in the politics of feminism on the one hand and the politics of class on the other. They focus rather on divisions between women, invoking a victimology of those who are the most oppressed.

It is perhaps relevant here that the issue has been more closely associated with radical than socialist feminism: to take just one indicator, you will find much more discussion of classism in the pages of the radical feminist journal *Trouble and Strife* than in the socialist influenced *Feminist Review*. For socialist feminists, the linking of women with class points to the complexity of political choice, to the ways that what women want as women may conflict with what women *and men* want as a class. For radical or revolutionary feminism it necessarily refers to differences among women.

When revolutionary feminists defined women as a 'sex class', they ruled mixed politics out of court, leaving class to be discussed in the vacuum of a women-only politics. And once the categorisation of all women as members of the same class lost its appeal – as was happening by the time of the 1979 Radical/Revolutionary Feminist Conference[55] – there was only one way forward. Having ruled out in advance what could be *one* of the differences – that working-class women have been allied in struggles with working-class *men* – your options are limited, you have one way to go. You take up the issue in terms of tensions between working- and middle-class feminists: you focus on individual behaviour and cultural control; you erect a hierarchy of privilege and suffering that leaves white, middle-class, and heterosexual feminists barely oppressed at all. The argument has travelled full circle. It starts from all women as a single sex-class, joined in common struggle against their enemy, the men. It moves on from this to acknowledge the very real differences in women's class positions, the problems we face when we pretend we are the same. It ends almost denying that women are oppressed as women, for if you inhabit that lucky segment that shares the privileges of the rulers, your oppression as a woman is virtually cancelled out.

Yet the real questions around class are surely those to do with divided loyalties: the lack of fit between the oppressions of gender and those of class or race; the risk that what we want for the one cuts across what we want for the others. Class matters, not because it gets in the way of us feeling the same, but because of the choices it suggests between the goals we pursue. It has been part of the politics of the contemporary women's movement that it challenges the notion of priority: the personal *is* political; we face the oppression of jobs and family and sexuality – the lot. The idea that some things are more pressing than others has always been used to put down the concerns of feminism ('wait till after the revolution – not just now, love') and in refusing this, feminists have subverted the language of choice. Yet the women's movement, as we have seen, *has* made its either/or choices, focussing on some issues to the relative, even total exclusion of others. The resulting absences have been most starkly raised in the context of racism, for when black women began to form their own organisations in the late

1970s, the relationship with feminism was highly contentious, partly because this was identified with 'luxury' concerns. As one woman commented:

> I think if you're a Black woman, you've got to begin with racism. It's not a choice, it's a necessity. There are a few Black women around now, who don't want to deal with that reality and prefer sitting around talking about their sexual preferences or concentrating on strictly women's issues like male violence. But the majority of Black women would see these kinds of things as 'luxury' issues. What's the point of taking on male violence if you haven't dealt with State violence? Or rape, when you can see Black people's bodies and lands being raped everyday by the system? If women want to sit around discussing who they go to bed with, that must be because it's the most important thing in their lives and that's all they want to deal with. In my mind, that's a privilege most of us don't have.[56]

As this so acutely reveals, it is hard to avoid the notion of priority, for it is difficult to engage with all issues at once. If you talk about one thing, you drown out another; when your time is spent in one campaign, you have less energy for another. Implicitly or explicitly you are making your choices, revealing what you find most important. And if this has been pointedly raised by the oppressions of race, it is equally relevant to questions of class.

Working-class feminism: Women against pit closures

It is informative here to look at the politics expressed by working-class women outside the movement, for the problems they have identified with feminism have little in common with the arguments inside. Take the unparalleled – and by virtually everyone unanticipated – phenomenon of Women Against Pit Closures, which burst onto the scene in 1984. When the miners' strike began in March of that year, the newspapers swept into action, publicising the views of those wives who wanted their men back at work. The tactic misfired, for it helped precipitate a nationwide network of miners' wives, miners' daughters, women in and around the mining communities, who organised in support of the strike.

The speed of its development seems to have amazed even those involved, for hundreds of women's groups sprung up in the first month of the strike. When a women's rally was held in Barnsley in May – a 'small encouraging rally' as those organising it expected[57] – it drew an exuberant mass of ten thousand women; marching and singing through the streets of Barnsley, they were led not by the traditional miners' brass band, but by the little girl drummers, the majorettes who are also a part of mining village tradition. By all accounts, that Civic Hall meeting was an overwhelming event.

The first activities fell into the traditional feminine fold: fund-raising, running food kitchens, arranging parties and trips for the children. Soon the women were encroaching on more masculine territory and joining the picketing of the pits. As the months of what was to prove a year long strike wore on, the women went further afield, taking their message to meetings up and down the country, travelling to Ireland, both North and the Republic, addressing huge rallies of trade unionists and socialists in virtually every country in Europe. In July 1984 they formed the national Women Against Pit Closures structure with representatives from all over the coalfields, an organisation which has continued in existence since the end of the strike.

Reflecting on the rapidity of its development, Jean McCrindle, treasurer of the national body, herself a lecturer at a trade union college and a woman with a long history of involvement both in mining community politics and in the women's movement, has commented that the movement must owe something to the previous spread of feminist ideas.[58] The more direct influence perhaps was the experience of involvement through Labour Party and Communist Party politics: one of the first groups to form, for example, was in Chesterfield, where women had worked together in Tony Benn's recent election campaign; another was in Barnsley, where a number of women were from labour or communist families, and where the nearby trade union college had already sparked off discussion on the relationship between the NUM and women.

Whatever the origins, the self-organisation of women was clearly a key part of what the movement was about. It was *their* groups, *their* rallies, the food kitchens were run by *them* and not the NUM, and when they first joined the picket lines it was often against the advice of NUM officials or members. No longer passive, the women could act, and as Lorraine Bowler put it in her speech at the Barnsley rally:

This fight does not just belong to the men, it belongs to us all ... In this country we aren't just separated as a class. We are separated as men and women. We, as women, have not often been encouraged to be involved actively in trade unions and organising. Organisation has always been seen as an area belonging to men. We are seen to be the domesticated element of a family. This for too many years has been the role expected of us. I have seen change coming for years and the last few weeks has seen it at its best. If this Government thinks its fight is only with the miners they are sadly mistaken. They are now fighting men, women and families.[59]

Asserting a place for the women was then part of the politics, but the impetus behind was supporting the men. The movement began in the women's refusal to be split from the men, and running through the campaign were two motifs that seem to mark its distance from contemporary feminism: the almost hero-worship of a man ('Arthur Scargill walks on water'); and the determination to fight for the family. Not surprisingly, those involved have felt themselves a long way from the women's movement. As Jean McCrindle has noted, 'there was a kind of fear of feminism ... for the first few months. A lot of women would say, "we're not feminists, we're nothing to do with those Greenham people. We're not lesbians".'[60] As at the time of the struggle for the vote, public images of feminism erected a barrier: remember the Guildswomen in the 1890s who were at pains to mark their difference from the 'goggle-eyed human ostrich, the exponent of women's rights who dresses as men and whose bearing so nearly resembles that of a man';[61] remember the difficulties the radical suffragists had in mobilising working-class women when faced with those ladies who 'kick, bite, shriek and spit'.[62] At both moments stereotypes were fostered by newspapers and word of mouth, and the power of the media is that much greater in our own age of TV. For Women Against Pit Closures the stereotypes were partly shifted in subsequent contacts with lesbian and gay groups who travelled to mining villages to give their support, in trips by some of the women's groups to Greenham Common, and in return visits by women involved with the politics of peace. But with all their willingness to acknowledge these allies from outside, 'most of the miners' wives feel very vehemently and still say quite vehemently, "we're not feminists" '.[63]

Thinking about this, we can see at least one link with the arguments on classism inside the movement: stereotypes breed on lifestyles, making the 'feminist' seem a species apart. In the pursuit of a new way of living, the women's movement created its own culture and it is one that can seem class-bound from both inside and out. But of the other arguments that have taken place *inside* the movement, we find little trace. Women in the mining communities are not complaining of the privileges of middle-class women: if privilege is invoked it is that of an entire class.

The point of greatest contact with contemporary feminism is perhaps over the changes the women talk of in their relations with men. With the women engaged in an endless round of meetings, pickets, food kitchens, trips and speeches, domestic work was either shared or else went to the wall. The very presence of the strike took the women out of the domestic sphere and brought the men back in. 'Being faced with small children on a daily basis, the miners have become more determined to fight for jobs for future generations. I've seen older men, not usually bothered with children, actually nurse youngsters while their parents eat their meal in peace.'[64] Many women have commented that after the strike they would not be going back to the old ways. 'Women have discovered during all this activity that we are not just wives any more. We're people too, and just as it's a different workforce going back to the pit, it's a different wife he will be coming home to.'[65]

The new sense of their own worth points to the oppressions in their previous existence, but few will express this as antagonism to the men.

> I think the men have changed a lot – they've got an awful lot more respect for the womenfolk than they ever used to have. Women I've known who've always been stuck at home and never doing anything and now the men are bursting with pride because they are out there speaking. 'That's my Mrs.' It's great. And the women's march – I think that was the thing that took everybody's breath away. We hadn't got any money – we just decided we were going to do it – and within a month we'd raised £23,000. The strike has given women a sense of their worth.[66]

> As women we can never be the same as we were. We no longer have the time to waste on such trivialities as housework or knitting. The important things for us are

other people's struggles and the things we now spend our time on are: Labour Party meetings, union meetings, joining others on their picket lines and fighting for the right of the victims of Thatcher.[67]

'Such trivialities as housework or knitting': it is reminiscent of remarks made in the women's movement in the previous decade, though interestingly enough this might have been criticised then as dismissive of working-class women. Spending our time on 'other people's struggles' strikes a novel note, for it was struggling against your *own* oppression that was so much a theme in women's liberation. Because it is grounded in what is so decisively a politics of class, the feminism of Women Against Pit Closures has its resonances with, but is not the same as the (already multi-variate) feminisms of the contemporary women's movement. Again to quote from Jean McCrindle:

Many of us have said in the women's movement that until there is a working-class women's movement, we won't know what it will – what the women who are part of it will want from it. We know the ideas of the women's movement are relevant to all women, but we don't know the forms and content of what they will take out of it and make their own. I think this movement has given us some kind of clues as to what these might be.[68]

What the next years will bring, both for Women Against Pit Closures and for women's politics as a whole, is hard to imagine, but we can be sure that class will pose us some problems. A hundred years ago it was liberalism that was the backdrop to feminism; this time round socialism took over that role. The resulting engagement has been continuous and troubled; even allowing for the selectivity of my account, the last fifteen years have been saturated with class – sometimes as anger, sometimes as anguish, sometimes as simplicity, other times as confusion.

Not then a movement innocent of difference, but one where class has stalked our endeavours. The effects have been varied, for on the wings of what seems like the same wish women have flown off in different directions, sometimes to focus on women at work, other times to emphasise women in the home. Relations with the labour movement have been recurrent but tangled – sometimes with what seems subservience to the language of class; other times with a defiant offensive. And whichever stance women have adopted, they have exposed themselves to criticism from inside and out: activists inside have questioned the privileges of middle-class sisters: those outside have seen it as too anti-men. None of this can be explained by the absence of class, for feminism today has been racked by its presence.

6 Out of Distortion: Into Confusion?

Standing back from the last two hundred years of feminist politics we cannot deny that class is a problem. The very way that women experience their womanhood has been conditioned by their place in the class structure which has meant not so much that some classes of women are more likely to be 'feminist' than others, but certainly that the problems they identify can vary by class. Too much work or too little? Too much femininity or not enough? Does the family constrain or support? Is independence an option, a necessity or what?

Comparing the situation today with what it was a hundred years ago, we can argue that women are more united than before. The imperatives of femininity are less class-bound than they were; the decline in domestic service means that most women are left with their problems with housework and children; the growth in female employment means that most of us are trying to fit in some job. But we are divided along the axis of full-time and part-time, separated into categories of professional, white collar, semi-skilled and unskilled, cut across by differences of race, age and marriage: women's working lives are far from the same. The fact that at every level in the job market we occupy positions below those of men with comparable skills provides only a tenuous link; as we go out to work in increasing numbers, we are stratified by our jobs in ways long familiar to the men. In the privacies of the household we may face the same problems; in the publicity of our jobs we are not all as one.

The positions women have taken up on major issues of political contention have not, as I hope I have shown, been *determined* by class, but different experiences have highlighted different aspects of oppression, and in both their priorities and their practice women have been formed by class. None of this is surprising, and indeed if anything is remarkable in the history of women's politics it is the extent of the engagement with issues of class. The focus on women has not proved the blinkers its critics suppose, for at virtually every moment in this history, the women's movement has acknowledged dilemmas of class. Sometimes this has served to shift the emphasis from one demand to another; sometimes it has surfaced as a hierarchy of oppression; sometimes it has been noted only to restate more firmly the fundamental unity of women. The engagement has not always been fruitful, but only the most jaundiced could say that class was ignored.

What has surprised me more in reflecting on this history is the way the admission of class creates extra problems, forcing our arguments into categories that confine. Thus one salutary lesson is that class has served to codify – and thereby simplify – what are genuine disagreements between women, leading to false dichotomies between 'middle-class' and 'working-class' views. The code itself has changed through time, for class has been invoked to what seem contradictory ends: sometimes to argue that issues of work are less important than issues of motherhood; sometimes to say that questions of sex pale into insignificance beside the burning concerns of unequal pay. Class so much structures our experience that we can almost always explain disagreements away by pointing up differences in our social position; claiming our own stance as the right one we can dismiss all the others as insensitive to class.

Yet the project we are engaged on overflows with choices and dilemmas and those who try to impose a single right-on line do us great disservice. When you look back over the history you may feel that *this* was the right move, *that* a mistake, but when all the campaigns and ideas and arguments stem from some aspect of women's experience, it does not help to see some as 'class-biased' while erecting the others into models to pursue. If you had been campaigning over women's right to employment in the 1870s and 1880s, what position would you have reached on protective legislation? If you had been working for women's right to vote in the 1900s, what choices would you have made between full adult suffrage and votes for women? If you had been agitating for improved conditions for mothers and children in the 1920s and 1930s, how quick would you have been to defend a woman's right to work?

In her recent reassessment of the relationship between feminism and puritanism, Sheila Jeffreys has portrayed the 'new feminists' of that era as almost traitors to their sex, arguing that their emphasis on motherhood consigned to oblivion the spinsters and the women who worked for a wage. 'In abandoning the fight for equality and embracing the endowment of motherhood, Rathbone betrayed the interests of spinsters, lesbians, and any women who wished to escape from unsatisfactory relationships with men.'[1] In the name of class I could well counter with the observation that Eleanor Rathbone and her followers were more in tune with the experiences of poorer women – but in truth there is no simple right or wrong. The disputes arise in contexts and a language we do not control, and they drag us into either/or choices where neither should do.

The very pervasiveness of women's oppression makes it hard to determine where to make our first stand, and we find ourselves beset by what seem inconsistent desires. When Zoë Fairbairns wrote her novel *Benefits*, a powerful and disturbing vision of what happens when the Government of National Regeneration introduces a payment to all mothers who stay at home to look after their children, she was writing out of what she felt were her own mutually contradictory opinions.[2] The mid-seventies arguments over wages for housework had left her head in a spin.

> 'Pay housewives and free them from dependence on their men,' said one group, 'It's a good idea.'
> 'Yes,' I thought, 'it is.'
> 'Don't pay housewives, it'll only institutionalise their position in the home,' said another group, 'it's a bad idea.'
> 'Yes,' I thought, 'it is.'[3]

The novel imagines what might happen if a British government introduced a wage for mothers, and it projects a horrific result. The single 'Benefit' replaces all previous welfare payments: no need for unemployment pay, for with the women back at the home, the men can be sure of finding a job; no need for social security or income supplements, for the needs of mothers and children are quite adequately met. The welfare state goes into reverse, and women's right to employment is explicitly denied. Yet Benefit does give women some space and, abandoning their husbands, many move into all female communities where they bring up their children together. The Family Party responds by making benefit selective and payable only to fit and dutiful mothers; as the scenario develops, Benefit is linked to terrifyingly eugenicist schemes. A contraceptive chemical is introduced into the water supply, and only the 'chosen' mothers can get the antidote that will make them once more fertile. Deformed babies are born, and the women go into revolt.

Yet the book deliberately leaves us with unresolved questions, as one of the leading characters warns against over-reaction to what Benefit had implied.

> 'That's what we've got to beware of today, sisters. Mistaking the way Benefit was exploited – and the horror that's come out of it – for the thing itself. Because what I'm going to do now is defend Benefit and I hope you'll hear me out. I'm not defending the reasons we were given it, or the way it let the Department of Family Welfare – sic, sic, sic! – think it had bought shares in our wombs – but the *principle* that people whose life's work is raising kids should be rewarded in the same way as people whose life's work is anything else, particularly as it's unlikely that that 'anything else' is more important or difficult than raising kids. It's a principle that our government's in the mood to yield, and I think that … yes, yes, whatever our attitudes to the government, whatever *alternatives* we're going to propose to government, we should keep it in the forefront of our minds. Because a social order that penalises good mothers for being good mothers won't survive and won't deserve to.[4]

Commenting on responses to the book, Zoë Fairbairns notes that for her the contradictions remain: on the one hand if you paid women for their work at home this would free them from a degrading dependence on male wages or the necessity to hold down two jobs; on the other hand a wage for housework could be used against women in horrific and controlling ways. 'What's missing,' she suggests, 'is a feminist response to motherhood and family life that is just enough and realistic enough to acknowledge that some women might actually want to live that way.'[5]

The problem in formulating feminist demands is that each change is only partial, and it loses its impact when isolated from others. I may believe that men and women should assume equal responsibility for child care, and that hours of paid work should be reduced to accommodate this need. But what then is my answer to those who point out that as things are, mothering is the one fulfilling area women still call their own – that as things are, having men bumbling around the house will make things worse before it can make them better? As things are, yes, and I cannot pretend to an unqualified confidence in my own solutions, for their very success would depend on a wide range of simultaneous tranformations. Along with Michèle Barrett and Mary McIntosh, I may favour 'the "clear break" model of divorce where any property is divided as soon as possible and there is no continuing obligation to provide maintenance, except for children until they start work', for maintenance to divorced wives simply assumes and reinforces our dependence on men.[6] But what then is my answer to those who point out that as things are, ex-wives will earn considerably less than ex-husbands, and that the former's disadvantages in the labour market are as much products of the marriage as the latter's superior chances? The counter-arguments may not budge me from my position, but they should at least alert me to the legitimate basis of alternative views.

This is not an argument for agnosticism, nor yet for cosy tolerance, but it *is* a case for taking seriously the grounds on which we disagree. And it is one of the difficulties class makes in our lives that it so often serves to relieve us of this task. Differences of opinion get overlaid by differences of class, and we stop too often at the veneer. We may note that it is middle-class women who typically argue one position, working-class women who argue the other; and then depending on where we place ourselves and our politics, we consider the matter is settled. Wages for housework, we might say, is the demand with most resonance for working-class women, for they have little hope of financial independence through work and few prospects for a job more fulfilling than motherhood. Those who condemn it as a trap are those already free: all right for some, but what about the others? Maintenance payments, we might argue, matter only for middle-class women, and for the rest are more trouble than they're worth: unless your ex-husband earns a considerable salary, you have to supplement your maintenance with social security – and if (as so often happens) the maintenance is not paid, you are left worse off than before. Which side of the fence you come down on depends, we may think, on your class.

When we can identify the arguments of our opponents with a

class position we have reason to distrust, our dilemmas seem easily resolved. We incline to packages of ideas, and class has proved a convenient label. 'Typically middle class', we find ourselves saying; or 'so very workerist' we mutter in despair. It is a way of saving ourselves time and effort, for instead of teasing out the complexities of the issues at stake, we can choose our positions by the calibre of our allies: if the wrong people support them, the ideas are at fault.

This kind of packaging bedevils all forms of political activity, leading us to reject what is good because of too close an association with what we believe to be bad. People are of course perverse enough to resist, but when you try to throw off the labels they stick on like glue. I once heard a working-class woman complain at a Labour Party meeting about the way that concern for the environment was thought to be a middle-class fad. 'Don't *we* care whether our children see trees?' The meeting warmed to her support, but in an anger that soon displaced itself into class condemnation. 'What right has the middle class to hijack this issue? Who are *they* to tell us that workers don't care?' The issue of the environment dropped from discussion, for the language of class can deprive us of words. Wanting to avoid error, we are often paralysed by fear of ending up in the wrong camp; when we doubt our way forward, we stick by those that we know.

Feminism has on the whole a worthy record in side-stepping such constraints, for when it introduces the conflicts of gender into a politics defined by class it necessarily changes the terrain. Picking its way through the minefield, it makes its novel connections: that poverty is female and not just working class; that trade unions are a problem for women as well as a scourge of employers; that sexual violence is no respector of class. The women's movement (both historically and now) has allowed us to forge new kinds of alliance, and in the process has disrupted the battle lines of before.

But as should be clear from the history of this movement, feminism has not been able to free itself completely, and because the divisions *between* women have often corresponded to their differences of class (never exclusively, but enough to keep them alive) we too have suffered from the packaging of ideas. Initiatives have been condemned or supported according to the class characters they have assumed, and our efforts to construct a well-rounded politics have suffered from this. The labelling is done by our opponents, but it is also done by ourselves. And it is for this reason most of all that I find the current discourse of privilege within women's movement politics so deeply disabling, for it promotes a simplistic approach to what are necessarily complex concerns. Neither of the two extremes now available to us will do: we cannot deduce our right-on feminism from an obsession with privilege; nor can we develop our 'woman-centered values' in isolation from a knowledge of class.

As Sheila Rowbotham has put it in a discussion of what women want:

> Values are not intact. And nobody has the patent. They can have radical and conservative meanings depending on political emphasis and historical context. Freedom, collectivity, difference, recognition can be used and balanced differently by popular movements of the right and left. Mothers and amazons can be recruited by both sides ... Our values, even in opposition, are part of existing culture. They are not just made by an effort of will. They come from our own often contradictory perceptions of where we find ourselves historically. A political idea, 'feminism' assumes a certain clarity, even programmes of action. But living a culture makes for confusion. A new combination of opposing ideas and a contesting culture of assumptions is vital for a political and social movement. But how do we define such values? Where should we concentrate our efforts; on establishing an alternative or taking it into the established order, for instance? Choices like these are of great strategic significance. They do not come easily.[7]

The choices for women are difficult and class must not act as our censor, for we need all the subtlety and imagination we can summon to find out the best way forward. To say this is not to say that class is irrelevant. It is precisely because class *does* matter that we face such problems. The varying positions women inhabit within the social order give them different kinds of opportunities, impose on them different kinds of inequalities, draw them into different strategies of political action. We cannot do without an awareness of class, and the feminism that celebrates only woman's identity as woman will breed its counterpart in the feminism that focuses exclusively on the oppressions of working-class women. Beyond this dichotomy lies the knowledge of contradiction: that women want and need different things at different times. Media images of feminists have presented us as if we have few things in mind: burn your bra, smash the family, emasculate the men. But the long history of women's struggle against oppression has been infinitely more varied – and infinitely more tortuous. The dilemmas we have faced have arisen in the context of a society divided by class and by race; sometimes distorted by class myopia; sometimes simplified by too-easy accusations of bias by class. The dilemmas remain.

Socialism and feminism and the dilemmas of class

For feminists involved in socialist politics, class has assumed a different dimension, for it is associated with what is orthodox, oppressive and male. At the beginning of the 1970s socialist feminists were often constrained by their inheritance, locked in a politics that could subsume gender to class. At this point, as Cynthia Cockburn has commented, if you were a socialist feminist 'it could safely be supposed that you did not see men-as-men as "the" or even "a" problem', for your emphasis would be on capitalism and the relations of class. As the emphasis shifted, 'an exception began to be made for male trade unionists, especially shop stewards and officers, who it became permissible to represent as an impediment. Not yet however our brothers in work.'[8] The final taboo was later broken, and as socialist feminists came to adopt a more 'radical' stance, the emancipation seemed complete. By 1979 Amanda Sebestyen was noting (with some irritation) that the strategies first developed by radical feminism were going through a 'laborious process of being sniffed over, repatented as "socialist" and certified acceptable ... I call myself a radical feminist and they call themselves socialist feminists. So what is going on?'[9] Throwing off more fully what seemed the shackles of class, socialist feminists were refusing its primacy over gender; the labour movement stood accused as a 'movement of men'.

Inside both unions and Labour Party this has surfaced in the arguments over the representation of women, and the resistance to feminism has strengthened the mood. The problem we find here is almost the obverse of the problem posed for feminism as a whole, for while in the wider arena it is the 'discovery' of difference that has claimed such attention, here class has nearly exhausted its credit. The labour movement has held tight to its masculine power and when Ann Pettifor (national organiser of the Women's Action

Committee) describes a stark scenario of women against men, she is giving voice to a frustration that many have shared.

> The labour movement's chauvinism is brutal in its determination to maintain male power within the institutions and organisations of the working class. It is a brutality not confined to one or other wing of the movement, to one or other faction. Labour women anxious to further the interests of working-class women are opposed by right-wing men and left-wing men; by gay men and 'straight' men; by the parliamentary male establishment and by the male rank-and-file; by black men and white men; by trade union leaders and by rank-and-file shop stewards.[10]

Class has been yoked to the supremacy of these men; its arguments are regarded with suspicion.

But the context in which this has occurred is a difficult one, for the more determined assault by socialist feminists coincided with the election – and subsequently re-election – of a more right-wing government than most of us had feared in our wildest of dreams. In partial reflection of this, socialists as a whole have fallen into a mode of reassessment and retreat, and all the old certainties are laid out for question. Is class politics outmoded? Is nationalisation a dead duck? Is it the 'have-nots' or 'haven't-got-enoughs' that matter? Do we defend the unions or curtail their powers? Do we speak for the producers or is it the consumers who count? And in the area that touches most acutely on feminist nerves, does orthodox class politics push aside as irrelevant those who are neither white nor male?

I do not wish to rehearse here the arguments that have raged within the Communist Party, where the very success of 'Thatcherism' was attributed by some to the bunker mentality of the left, and where the anachronisms of class were held partly responsible.[11] But the issues raised in this debate have simmered through the whole of the labour and socialist movement, and the arguments of feminism help bring them to the boil. In pursuit of a radical egalitarian future, many women have questioned the orthodoxies of class. Will the arguments be highjacked to a more limited end?

When the battle over the future of the coal-fields broke in 1984, feminists might well have retreated to an agnostic or critical stance: machismo on the picket lines is not our scene; fighting for the family is hardly our line. As it turned out, feminists from all over rallied in support, but the transition was eased by the development of women's support groups throughout the mining communities, and what if these women had been less determined? Would we then have withheld our support, distanced ourselves from yet another tedious masculine struggle, reminded ourselves of the chauvinism of mining existence, criticised the leadership for its autocratic ways? And what do we think of it now, when the NUM has refused affiliate status to Women Against Pit Closures, failed to give substance to its oft-repeated praise?

Inside the Labour Party, the so-called 'hard left' of the Militant Tendency has encapsulated an orthodoxy that feminists have attacked. It regards the politics of the women's movement as 'bourgeois'; it operates with that hierarchical efficiency the women's movement has so fundamentally refused; it sees class as the issue and hardly anything else counts. Few of those influenced by the women's movement can feel much sympathy for its practice and goals. But wrapped up in the argument for expelling Militant supporters is a cosmetic cleansing of unpopular ideas, and if as a feminist I would like to see Militant out, as a socialist I am treading on dangerous terrain.

Many women involved in socialist politics have argued that there is no necessary conflict between the two projects, that an impoverished version that denies women's interests discredits the socialist ideal. Feminism then appears as the guarantor of our future: it represents democracy, equality, our real living needs. And if in pursuit of this future we have to unmask what was once thought of as 'good' socialist practice (the knee-jerk defence of all trade union struggles, the posturing of 'radicals' who try to prove their intent), the ultimate gains will benefit all. Far from conflicting with the politics of class, feminism will revitalise its ideals.

The argument is attractive – and perhaps this is why I doubt its full truth. It follows a pattern traced out in many discussions within contemporary socialism, and it looks too much like trying to have it both ways. A parallel would be the (very legitimate and important) criticisms socialists have made of the welfare state, where they have pointed to the failures of accountability; the naive assumption that bigger is better – whether the object is a hospital or a school or a housing estate; the way that democracy has been sacrificed to bureaucratic control. Having criticised so trenchantly the practices of post-war welfare, socialists might well have found themselves in turmoil when even those inadequacies were threatened with the knife. Faced with major cuts in public spending, how much could we afford the luxury of complaints? We might have our reservations about the health service, the schools, social services, council housing programmes – the whole apparatus of the welfare state – but perhaps for the moment we should swallow our murmurs, perhaps we should rally just to defend?

Characteristically in the 1970s and '80s, socialists have refused this dilemma, arguing that even defence must admit past mistakes. Disillusion with the health service, it has been argued, has gone so far that no one will campaign in its support unless the campaigns are based on criticisms of what went before. Parental dissatisfaction with the schools runs so deep that no one will defend education unless it promises to improve. Council tenants are so fed up with their landlord that they will hold back support until there is change. The argument is a courageous one, and it lies behind some of the more imaginative initiatives of recent years: no point retreating to what you know is inadequate; if you want to win out you must push for much more.

The same logical structure underlies what many feminists (including myself) have argued in the socialist context; no hope of winning if we stick by the old; transformed by feminism we have at least a chance. The argument promises to dissolve our dilemmas, but in practice the schizophrenia remains. Take the problem of weaving the needs of women into policies on employment. Feminist inside both Labour and Communist Parties have argued extensively that we need to do more than restore what is past: that 'full employment' must address the working lives of women, tackling the inequalities between women and men. In pressing for this wider vision, feminists have claimed it will capture more hearts, arguing that the greater the ambition the more widespread the support. Yet of course this could prove mere wishful thinking: certainly as arguments over economics carry on their way, the feminist 'critique' has seemed utopian and unreal. Women argue for a major restructuring of working hours that would transform the pattern between household and jobs; men turn their attention to controlling the banks.[12] It has proved virtually impossible to shift the terrain, and while this demonstrates once again the dominance of men, it is depressing to have to harp on this point.

We have much further to go before we can claim all the answers, and the journey is more solitary than it would have been before. As the national structures of the Women's Liberation Movement have fallen away, socialist feminists are less challenged by other women's perceptions, less engaged with internal feminist debate. The dialogue that takes place is often with those who may question our most basic commitment, and then each obstacle we encounter reinforces our beliefs; it does not encourage us to think through our ideas. It is in this sense both revealing and disturbing that feminism in the labour movement has focussed on issues of representation rather than policy – as though we know what we want if we could just get the men to listen. In truth we have many unanswered questions – as most feminists will admit once the men are away – but the resistance we encounter swallows our energies, taking us from work we still have to do. For women operating in a primarily socialist rather than feminist context this is one of the dangers we face: it can make our feminism a 'given' and single-minded concern. We see ourselves guardians of a potion with restorative powers – the magic that can reverse any socialist decline. This very confidence can block us in further work on our vision, leaving us poorly equipped for the politics of the day.

The parallel difficulty relates to the timescale, for if ultimately feminism *must* hold many answers, the ultimate is not the stuff of which politics is made. In campaigning for sexual equality inside the labour movement women face a multitude of strategic and tactical questions, and our feminism is no slide rule from which we read off the answers. Every ward meeting and every union meeting throws up its dilemma, and compromise and choice seem the name of the game. From streetlighting to nurseries to jobs to whatever, there are always good reasons for opposite views. Softer streetlighting may reduce hazards for cars and therefore pedestrians, but they increase the dangers for women at night. More money for nurseries means less for something else. More offices open up jobs for women, but they play into the hands of property speculators. New technology can mean openings for the employment of women but it often threatens the jobs of the men who are there. We can construct a logic in which the dilemmas dissolve, but we still have to grapple with short-term demands.

Sometimes there is an immediate and positive unity, as with the question of conductors on buses or guards on trains, where the union defence of jobs meshes neatly with women's concern for safety, and the problems of getting on and off a bus with buggy and baby and shopping add extra weight to the argument for retaining conductors. But more often than not there is some kind of choice, with the solutions neither obvious nor simple. In the short term that is our inevitable horizon, gender and class can seem to point different ways. And if we are to get beyond what I myself experience as schizophrenia (sometimes my socialist hat, sometimes my feminist one) we can only do so if we admit these tensions we face.

I would love to end with a long list of imperatives: to set out, for example, how feminists should relate to a labour movement under stress; what they should say when they call for higher wages for nursery workers and are reminded that some men are low paid too; what they should do when resource constraints seem to impose a choice between more aid to the Third World and more money on social services; how they should respond to women's desire to stay at home with their children without sacrificing the demands of a woman's right to work. But on these and all the other choices that confront us, easy answers are not the solution – confusion may be the reality we have to force ourselves to face. What matters is that we acknowledge our divided loyalties, do not try to deny them in the confidence of our cause. We have to beware of claiming that feminism has the answers, for we are engaged on a project that must continue to grow.

Notes

1 Liberation for All or Just a Few?

1. Juliet Mitchell, 'Women and Equality', p.387, in Juliet Mitchell and Ann Oakley (eds) *The Rights and Wrongs of Women*, Penguin, London, 1976.
2. Olive Banks, *Faces of Feminism*, pp.4-5, Martin Robertson, Oxford, 1981.
3. Marion Ramelson, *The Petticoat Rebellion*, p.32, Lawrence and Wishart, London, 1972.
4. Michèle Barrett, 'Marxism-Feminism and the Work of Karl Marx', p.202, in Betty Matthews (ed) *Marx: A Hundred Years On*, Lawrence and Wishart, London, 1983.
5. Sheila Rowbotham, *Woman's Consciousness, Man's World*, p.12, Penguin, London, 1973.
6. Frankie Rickford, *Guardian Women's Page*, 15 August 1984.
7. David Bouchier, *The Feminist Challenge*, p.56, Macmillan, London, 1983.
8. Frankie Rickford, op.cit.
9. See for example Hazel Carby, 'White Women Listen! Black Feminism and the Boundaries of Sisterhood', in Centre for Contemporary Cultural Studies, *The Empire Strikes Back: Race and Racism in 70s Britain*, Hutchinson, London, 1982; Valerie Amos and Pratibha Parmar, 'Challenging Imperial Feminism', *Feminist Review*, No.17, 1984.
10. Michèle Barrett and Mary McIntosh, 'Ethnocentrism and Socialist-Feminist Theory', p.24, *Feminist Review*, No. 20, 1985.
11. Anne Phillips, *Hidden Hands*, Pluto Press, London, 1983.

12. Marlene Packwood, 'The Colonel's Lady and Judy O'Grady: Class in the Women's Liberation Movement', *Trouble and Strife*, No.1, 1983.
13. ibid., p.10.
14. Mary Daly, *Gyn/Ecology*, Beacon Press, Boston, 1978; Women's Press, London; Dale Spender, *Women of Ideas*, Routledge and Kegan Paul, London, 1982.
15. Angela Davis, *Women Race and Class*, The Women's Press, London, 1982.
16. ibid., p.30.
17. ibid., p.53.
18. ibid., p.84.
19. ibid., p.81.
20. ibid., pp.115-6.

2   Class Matters

1. Contemporary marxism is more wary of such a solution, and for recent attempts to engage with the categories of middle and working class see N. Abercrombie and J. Urry, *Capital, Labour and the Middle Classes*, Allen and Unwin, London, 1983, or John Westergaard, 'The Once and Future Class', in James Curran (ed) *The Future of the Left*, Polity Press, Oxford, 1984.
2. Catherine Hakim, 'Sexual Division within the Labour Force: Occupational Segregation' *Employment Gazette*, November 1978; 'Job Segregation: Trends in the 1970s', *Employment Gazette*, December 1981.
3. In the literature this is known as the dual labour market theory, and a key article is R.D. Barron & G.M. Norris, 'Sexual Divisions and the Dual Labour Market' in Diana Leonard Barker and Sheiler Allen (eds) *Dependence and Exploitation in Work and Marriage*, Longman, London, 1976. For a critical discussion see Veronica Beechey, 'Women and Production: a Critical Analysis of some Sociological Theories of Women's Work', in Annette Kuhn and AnnMarie Wolpe (eds) *Feminism and Materialism*, Routledge and Kegan Paul, London, 1978.
4. For a discussion of this theory see for example Irene Bruegel, 'Women as a Reserve Army of Labour: a Note on Recent British Experience', *Feminist Review*, no.3, 1979.
5. The implications of the resulting 'family wage' are discussed (though not from a perspective that relies exclusively on the effects of capital) in Michèle Barrett and Mary McIntosh, 'The "Family Wage": Some Problems for Socialists and Feminists', *Capital and Class*, no.11, 1980.
6. See for example: Barbara Taylor, ' "The Men are as Bad as Their

Masters ..." Socialism, Feminism and Sexual Antagonism in the London Tailoring Trade in the Early 1830s', *Feminist Studies*, 5, no.1, 1979; Heidi Hartmann, 'Capitalism, Patriarchy and Job Segregation by Sex', in Zillah Eisenstein (ed) *Capitalist Patriarchy and the Case for Socialist Feminism*, Monthly Review, New York, 1979; Sarah Boston, *Women Workers and the Trade Unions*, Davis-Poynter, London, 1980; Cynthia Cockburn, *Brothers: Male Dominance and Technological Change*, Pluto Press, London, 1983.

7. Quoted in Taylor, op.cit.

8. Boston, op.cit., p.54.

9. ibid., p.79.

10. Heidi Hartmann, 'The Unhappy Marriage of Marxism and Feminism: Towards a More Progressive Union', *Capital and Class*, no.8, 1979.

11. Elizabeth Wilson and Angela Weir, 'The British Women's Movement', pp.102-103, *New Left Review*, no.148, 1984.

12. Abercrombie and Urry, op.cit.

13. John Westergaard, op.cit, p.83.

14. ILEA, *Race, Sex and Class: 1. Achievement in Schools*, Inner London Education Authority, London, 1983. The major post-war study of class in education is A.H. Halsey, A.F. Heath and J.M. Ridge, *Origins and Destinations*, Clarendon, Oxford, 1980.

15. J.H. Goldthorpe with C. Llewellyn and C. Payne, *Social Mobility and Class Structure in Modern Britain*, Clarendon, Oxford, 1980.

16. Frank Parkin, *Class Inequality and Political Order*, p.14, MacGibbon and Kee, London, 1977.

17. Elizabeth Garnsey, 'Women's Work and Theories of Class and Stratification', in A. Giddens and D. Held (eds) *Classes, Power and Conflict*, Macmillan, London, 1982; Michelle Stanworth, 'Women and Class Analysis: A Reply to John Goldthorpe', *Sociology*, 18.2, May 1984; Anthony Heath and Nicky Britten, 'Women's Jobs Do Make a Difference: A Reply to Goldthorpe', *Sociology*, 18.4, November 1984.

18. Stanworth, op.cit., p.164.

19. John Goldthorpe, 'Women and Class Analysis: In Defence of the Conventional View', *Sociology*, 17.4, November 1983.

20. Stanworth, op.cit.; Marilyn Porter, *Home, Work and Class Consciousness*, Manchester University Press, Manchester, 1983.

21. A. Giddens, *The Class Structure of the Advanced Societies*, p.288, Hutchinson, London 1973.

22. Jean Martin and Ceridwen Roberts, *Women and Employment: A Lifetime Perspective*, table 2.6, HMSO, London, 1984.

3   Classing the Women and Gendering the Class

1. Virginia Woolf, in Margaret Llewelyn Davies (ed) *Life As We Have Known It*, p.xxxi, Virago, London, 1977 (first published 1931).
2. E.P. Thompson, *The Making of the English Working Class*, p.9, Penguin, London, 1968.
3. J.D. Milne, *Industrial and Social Position of Women in the Middle and Lower Ranks*, p.141, London, 1857.
4. ibid., p.146.
5. Catherine Hall, 'The Early Formation of Victorian Domestic Ideology', in Sandra Burman (ed) *Fit Work For Women*, Croom Helm, London, 1979.
6. Gareth Stedman Jones, *Languages of Class: Studies in English Working Class History 1832-1982*, Cambridge University Press, London, 1983.
7. Hall, op.cit., p.15.
8. cited in I. Pinchbeck, *Women Workers and the Industrial Revolution 1750-1850*, p.35, Virago, London, 1981 (first published 1930).
9. Hall, op.cit.; Leonore Davidoff, 'The Separation of Home From Work? Landladies and Lodgers in Nineteenth and Twentieth Century England', in Burman, op.cit.
10. Elizabeth Gaskell, *North and South*, p.214, Penguin, London, 1970. (first published 1854-5).
11. J.D. Milne, op.cit., p.23.
12. I. Pinchbeck, op.cit.; J. Kitteringham 'Country Work Girls in Nineteenth Century England' in R. Samuel (ed) *Life and Labour*, Routledge and Kegan Paul, London, 1975.
13. Lee Holcombe, *Victorian Ladies At Work*, p.4, David and Charles, London, 1973.
14. See Margaret Hewitt, *Wives and Mothers in Victorian Industry*, Greenwood Press, Connecticut, 1975 (first published 1958).
15. ibid., ch.2.
16. ibid., ch.8 for discussion of the statistics on infant mortality.
17. Michael Anderson, *Family Structure in Nineteenth Century Lancashire*, Cambridge University Press, 1971; also John Foster, *Class Struggle and the Industrial Revolution*, Weidenfeld and Nicolson, London, 1974.
18. Hewitt, op.cit., ch.9; Anderson, op.cit., ch.6.
19. Kitteringham, op.cit.
20. Angela V. John, *By the Sweat of Their Brow: Women Workers at Victorian Coal Mines*, Croom Helm, London, 1980.
21. Christina Walkley, *The Ghost in the Looking Glass*, Peter Owen, London, 1981. Thomas Hood's 'Song of the Shirt' was published in Punch in 1843, establishing a tradition of depicting the seamstress as sad but refined.

22. Davidoff, op.cit., Sally Alexander, 'Women's Work in Nineteenth Century London, in J. Mitchell and A. Oakley (eds) *The Rights and Wrongs of Women*, Penguin, London, 1976.

23. It is particularly notable that infant mortality rates could be as high and sometimes even higher in middle-class areas. See Patricia Branca, *Silent Sisterhood: Middle Class Women in the Victorian Home*, ch.6, Croom Helm, London, 1975.

24. See B. Ehrenreich and D. English, *For Her Own Good: 150 Years of the Experts' Advice to Women*, Pluto Press, London, 1979, and Branca, op.cit.

25. Thus in the 1860s the Contagious Diseases Acts were introduced to control venereal disease among soldiers and sailors; they effectively exposed any working-class woman who lived in the area under their jurisdiction to arbitrary and compulsory examination for veneral disease. See Chapter Four.

26. Judith Walkowitz, *Prostitution and Victorian Society: Women, Class and the State*, Cambridge University Press, London, 1980.

27. Florence Nightingale, 'Cassandra', in Ray Strachey, *The Cause*, p.401, Virago, London, 1978.

28. ibid., p.408.

29. Cited in R. McWilliams-Tulberg, 'Women and Degrees at Cambridge University 1862-1897', in Martha Vicinus (ed) *A Widening Sphere: Changing Roles of Victorian Women*, Indiana University Press, Bloomington, 1977.

30. Geoffrey Crossick, 'The Emergence of the Lower Middle Class in Britain: a Discussion', p.13, in Crossick (ed) *The Lower Middle Class in Britain 1870-1914*, Croom Helm, London, 1977.

31. Branca, op.cit., p.44.

32. Crossick, op.cit., p.63.

33. Branca, op.cit., p.5.

34. George Gissing, *The Odd Women*, London, 1893.

35. Sarah Hartland, mathematics lecturer at Newnham, 1884, quoted in A. James Hammerton, 'Feminism and Female Emigration 1861-1886' in Vicinus, op.cit.

36. Holcombe, op.cit., p.55.

37. Bessie Rayner Parkes, 1860, quoted in Hammerton, op.cit., p.55.

38. Hammerton, op.cit.

39. Holcombe, op.cit., appendix 1.

40. Louisa M. Hubbard, *Work For Ladies in Elementary Schools*, p.iv, London, 1872.

41. Holcombe, op.cit., p.35.

42. Frances Widdowson, *Going Up Into The Next Class: Women and Elementary School Training*, p.47, Women's Research and Resources Centre Publications: Explorations in Feminism no.7, London, 1980.

43. Hubbard, op.cit., p.14.
44. Widdowson, op.cit., p.33.
45. ibid., p.49.
46. Hubbard, op.cit., p.7.
47. Widdowson, op.cit., p.30.
48. Holcombe, op.cit., appendix 2.
49. quoted in Holcombe, op.cit., p.78.
50. ibid. p.107.
51. ibid., appendix 3.
52. Crossick, op.cit., p.104.
53. A later example of this genre is H.G. Wells' *Ann Veronica* 1909, Virago, 1980.
54. Holcombe, op.cit., p.172.
55. Ruth Adam, *A Woman's Place 1910-1975*, p.19, Chatto and Windus, London, 1975.
56. Clara E. Collet, *The Economic Position of Educated Working Women*, p.6, South Place Ethical Society, London, 1890.
57. Frances Martin, 'A College For Working Women', in Carol Bauer and Laurence Ritt (eds) *Free And Enobled*, p.133, Pergamon Press, Oxford, 1979.
58. quoted in Holcombe, op.cit., p.19.
59. Crossick, op.cit., introduction.
60. Virginia Woolf, 'Professions For Women' in Virginia Woolf, *Women And Writing*, p.58, The Women's Press, London, 1979.
61. Maud Pember Reeves, *Round About A Pound A Week*, 1913, reprinted Virago, London, 1979; Clementina Black (ed) *Married Women's Work*, 1915, reprinted Virago, London, 1983; Margaret Llewelyn Davies (ed) *Maternity: Letters From Working Women*, 1915, reprinted Virago, London, 1978.
62. quoted in Anderson, op.cit., p.77.
63. Black, op.cit., p.136.
64. ibid., p.3.
65. Pember Reeves, op.cit., p.61.
66. ibid. p.23.
67. Quoted in Elizabeth Roberts, *A Woman's Place: On Oral History of Working-Class Women 1890-1940*, p.112, Basil Blackwell, Oxford, 1984.
68. ibid, p.2.
69. quoted in Gail Braybon, *Women Workers in the First World War*, p.48, Croom Helm, London, 1981.
70. ibid., p.163.
71. ibid., ch.7.
72. ibid., p.193.
73. Pam Taylor, 'Daughters and Mothers – Maids and Mistresses: Domestic Service Between the Wars', in J. Clarke, C. Critcher, R.

Johnson (eds) *Working Class Culture*, Hutchinson University Library, London, 1979.

74. Jane Lewis, *Women In England 1870-1950*, p.6, Wheatsheaf, Sussex, 1984.
75. ibid., p.18.
76. ibid., p.15.
77. Braybon, op.cit., p.217.
78. ibid., ch.7.
79. Lewis, op.cit., p.15.
80. ibid., p.7.
81. Jean Martin and Cerdiwen Roberts, *Women And Employment: A Lifetime Perspective*, table 2.6, HMSO, London, 1984. These figures are incomplete as they exclude homeworkers.
82. Gail Braybon has suggested that this divide was emerging even in the inter-war years.
83. Martin and Robert, op.cit., table 3.2.
84. ibid., table 3.1.
85. ibid., ch.9.
86. ibid., table 3.2.
87. 'Ethnic origin and economic status', table 6, *Employment Gazette*, Vol 91, No.10, October 1983.
88. Martin and Roberts, op.cit., ch.3.
89. Barbro Hoel, 'Contemporary Clothing "Sweatshops": Asian Female Labour and Collective Organisation', p.86, in Jackie West (ed) *Work, Women and the Labour Market*, Routledge and Kegan Paul, London, 1982.
90. Annie Phizaclea, 'Migrant Women and Wage Labour: the Case of West Indian Women in Britain', p.104, in West (ed) op.cit.
91. Michèle Barrett and Mary McIntosh, 'Ethnocentrism and Socialist-Feminist Theory', p.31, *Feminist Review*, No.20, 1985.
92. Phizacklea, op.cit.
93. Elizabeth Garnsey, 'Women's Work and Theories of Class and Stratification' in A. Giddens and D. Held (eds) *Classes, Power and Conflict*, Macmillan, London, 1982; Michelle Stanworth, 'Women and Class Analysis: a Reply to John Goldthorpe', *Sociology*, 18, 2, (1984).
94. Martin and Roberts, op.cit., table 10.16.
95. Anna Pollert, *Girls, Wives and Factory Lives*, Macmillan, London, 1981; Sallie Westwood, *All Day Every Day*, Pluto Press, London, 1984.
96. Westwood, op.cit., p.10.
97. ibid., p.159.
98. ibid., p.62.
99. ibid., pp. 62-3.
100. Sue Sharpe, *'Just Like a Girl': How Girls Learn to be Women*, p.154,

Penguin, London, 1976.
101. Ruth Cavendish, *Women On The Line*, p.122, Routledge and Kegan Paul, London, 1982.
102. Beatrix Campbell, *Wigan Pier Revisited*, p.65, Virago, London, 1984.
103. ibid., pp 63-4.
104. MORI poll 'Family Matters', *Sunday Times*, April, 1982.

4   Unity Threatened by Difference

1. *Englishwoman's Review*, May 15, 1876.
2. Christine de Pizan, *The Book of the City of Ladies*, Picador, London, 1983 (first published 1405).
3. Quoted in Juliet Mitchell, 'Women and Equality', p.389, in Mitchell and Oakley, op. cit.
4. ibid., p.387.
5. Mary Wollstonecraft, *Vindication of the Rights of Woman*, first published 1792, p.81, Penguin, London, 1975.
6. This is made particularly clear in Cora Kaplan's essay, 'Wild Nights', in *Formations of Pleasure*, Routledge and Kegan Paul, London, 1983.
7. Quoted in Ramelson, op.cit., p.58.
8. Wollstonecraft, op.cit., p.170.
9. This is Cora Kaplan's evocative phrase. See Kaplan, op.cit. p.28.
10. John Stuart Mill, 'The Subjection of Women', p.427, in J.S. Mill, *Three Essays*, Oxford University Press, London, 1975.
11. ibid., p.445.
12. ibid., p.448.
13. Harriet Taylor, 'Enfranchisement of Women' in Alice Rossi (ed) *J.S. Mill and Harriet Taylor Mill: Essays on Sex Equality*, p.105. University of Chicago Press, Chicago, 1970.
14. Quoted in A. Rosen, *Rise Up Women!*, p.8, Routledge and Kegan Paul, London, 1974.
15. Bessie Rayner Parkes, 'The Market for Educated Female Labour', *The English Woman's Journal*, p.149, Nov. 1859.
16. Bessie Rayner Parkes, 'What Can Educated Women Do?', *The English Woman's Journal*, p.293n., Jan. 1860.
17. Cited in Mabel Atkinson, *The Economic Foundations of the Women's Movement*, p.13n., Fabian Tract no. 175, June 1914.
18. The story of the campaign is told in Lee Holcombe, *Wives and Property*, University of Toronto Press, Toronto, 1983.
19. See Walkowitz, op.cit.
20. Quoted in Walkowitz, op.cit. p.130.
21. Angela V. John, *By The Sweat Of Their Brow*, Croom Helm, London, 1980.

22. Jill Liddington and Jill Norris, *One Hand Tied Behind Us*, Virago, London, 1978.

23. Holcombe, op.cit., p.66.

24. ibid., p.160.

25. ibid., p.117.

26. Margaret Hewitt, op.cit.

27. Ray Strachey, *The Cause*, p.238, Virago, London, 1978, (first published 1928).

28. See John, op.cit.

29. *Englishwoman's Review*, June 15, 1887.

30. Quoted in Strachey, op.cit., p.237.

31. *Englishwoman's Review*, Feb 15, 1886.

32. Quoted in John, op.cit., p.153.

33. For a more detailed account of this period, see Sarah Boston, *Women Workers and the Trade Unions*, Davis-Poynter, London, 1980.

34. John, op.cit., p.149.

35. Ellen Mappen, *Helping Women At Work: The Women's Industrial Council 1889-1914*, p.12, Hutchinson/Explorations in Feminism Collective, London, 1985.

36. ibid., p.19.

37. See Barbara Taylor, *Eve and the New Jerusalem*, Virago, London, 1983.

38. See Liddington and Norris. op.cit.

39. ibid. pp.239-240.

40. ibid. p.240.

41. Quoted in Jean Gaffin and David Thoms, *Caring and Sharing: The Centenary History of the Co-operative Women's Guild*, p.20, Co-operative Union Ltd, 1983.

42. Lewis, op.cit., p.91.

43. For the full account of this period of working-class feminism see Liddington and Norris, op.cit.; and Jill Liddington, *The Life and Times of a Respectable Rebel: Selina Cooper 1864-1946*, Virago, London, 1984.

44. *Burnley Co-operative Record*, Oct 1896, quoted in Liddington, op.cit., p.96.

45. The WCG continued to express worries about how far proposed suffrage extensions would affect the married working-class women it spoke for, but by the 1900s it had committed itself to the struggle. See Liddington, op, cit., ch.9.

46. Elizabeth Robins, *The Convert*, The Women's Press, London, 1980, (first published 1907).

47. Liddington, op.cit., p.145.

48. Hannah Mitchell, *The Hard Way Up*, p.126, Virago, London, 1977.

49. Liddington and Norris, op.cit., pp.181-183.

50. Quoted in Mitchell, op.cit., p.126.

51. Eva Gore-Booth on behalf of the Lancashire Women Textile Workers' Representation Committee to Mrs Fawcett, 25.10.1906. Quoted in Liddington and Norris, op.cit. pp.205-6.

52. Olive Schreiner, *Women and Labour*, Virago, London, 1978, (first published 1911).

53. ibid., p.82.

54. ibid., p.22.

55. ibid., p.200.

56. Atkinson, op.cit.

57. ibid., p.7.

58. ibid., p.13.

59. ibid., pp.14-15

60. ibid., p.16.

61. Gaffin and Thoms, op.cit., pp.48-51. The grant was withdrawn from 1914 to 1918.

62. Margaret Cole, *Women Of Today*, pp. 121-122, Book For Libraries Press, New York, 1968, (first published 1938).

63. Caroline Rowan, 'Women in the Labour Party 1906-1920', p.80, *Feminist Review*, no.12, 1982.

64. Lewis, op.cit., p.102.

65. The new feminism is discussed in Olive Banks, op.cit., ch. 10; Eleanor Rathbone's arguments over the family wage are taken up in Hilary Land, 'The Family Wage', *Feminist Review*, no.6, 1980.

66. Pember Reeves, op.cit.; Llewelyn Davies, op.cit.

67. Dora Russell, *The Tamarisk Tree, Vol I*, pp.175-6, Virago, London, 1977.

68. ibid., p.180.

69. Eleanor Rathbone, *The Disinherited Family*, p.44, Allen and Unwin, London, 1947.

70. Denise Riley, *War in the Nursery*, p.180, Virago, London, 1983.

71. ibid.

72. ibid. p.180.

73. ibid. p.184.

5 When Sisters Fall Out

1. 'A Short History of the Socialist Current within the British Women's Liberation Movement', p.5, *Scarlet Women* 4, 1977.

2. London Socialist Woman Group, *The Night-Cleaners' Campaign*, p.11, London 1971.

3. Union of Women For Liberation, *On The Working Women's Charter*, p.1, London, 1975.

4. Sheila Rowbotham, 'The Beginnings of Women's Liberation in Britain', 1972, reprinted in *Dreams and Dilemmas*, Virago, London, 1983; Anna Coote and Beatrix Campbell, *Sweet Freedom*, Pan,

London, 1982; David Bouchier, *The Feminist Challenge*, Macmillan, London, 1983.

5. May Hobbs, *Born To Struggle*, Quartet, London, 1973.
6. *Women's Newspaper*, no.1, 6 March 1971.
7. Alix Kates Shulman, *Burning Questions*, p.306, Fontana, London, 1980.
8. Mica Nava, 'From Utopian to Scientific Feminism? Early Feminist Critiques of the Family', pp.72-3, in Lynne Segal (ed) *What Is To Be Done About The Family?*, Penguin, London, 1983.
9. Jeanette Mitchell, 'Some Notes on the Second National Working Women's Charter Conference', p.18 *Scarlet Women* 4, 1977.
10. *Scarlet Women* 4, p.11. 1977.
11. Mariarosa Dalla Costa, 'Women and the Subversion of the Community', p.47. *The Power of Women and the Subversion of the Community*, Falling Wall Press, London, 1972.
12. For a very readable summary of the debate see Eva Kaluzynska, 'Wiping the Floor with Theory – a Survey of Writings on Housework', *Feminist Review*, no.6, 1980. Maxine Molyneux summarises subsequent criticisms in her 'Beyond the Domestic Labour Debate', *New Left Review*, no.116, 1979.
13. Letter in *WIRES*, no.43, January 1978.
14. *Spare Rib* 89, December 1979.
15. *Spare Rib* 87, October 1979.
16. Kate Millett, *Sexual Politics*, Sphere, London, 1971.
17. Shulamith Firestone, *The Dialectic of Sex*, Jonathan Cape, London, 1971.
18. Amanda Sebestyen, 'Tendencies in the Movement: Then and Now', p.22, *Feminist Practice: Notes from the Tenth Year!*, In Theory Press, London, 1979.
19. Sheila Jeffreys, 'The Need For Revolutionary Feminism', reprinted in *Scarlet Women* 5, 1977.
20. ibid, p.12.
21. Jalna Hanmer, Cathy Lunn, Sheila Jeffreys, Sandra McNeil, 'Sex-class; Why is it important to call women a class?', p.8, reprinted in *Scarlet Women* 5, 1977.
22. Coote and Campbell, op.cit., pp.40-42.
23. Report by Lorna Mitchell, p.26, *Spare Rib* 62, September 1977.
24. Leeds Revolutionary Feminist Group, 'Political Lesbianism: The Case Against Heterosexuality', reprinted in *Love Your Enemy? The Debate Between Heterosexual Feminism and Political Lesbianism*, Onlywomen Press, London, 1981.
25. 'Ever Wilde', *Working Class Women's Liberation Newsletter*, Summer 1979.
26. Sheila Rowbotham, Lynne Segal, Hilary Wainwright, *Beyond the Fragments*, London, 1979.

27. Anna Coote, 'The AES: a New Starting Point', *New Socialist*, no 2, 1981; Jean Gardiner and Sheila Smith, 'Feminism and the Alternative Economic Strategy', *Socialist Economic Review*, Merlin, London, 1982; Anne Phillips, *Hidden Hands* Pluto Press, London, 1983.

28. Michèle Barrett and Mary McIntosh, 'The "Family Wage": Some Problems for Socialists and Feminists', *Capital and Class*, No.11, 1980; Hilary Land, 'The Family Wage', *Feminist Review*, no.6, 1980.

29. Anne Phillips and Barbara Taylor, 'Sex and Skill: Notes Towards a Feminist Economics', *Feminist Review*, No.6, 1980; Heidi Hartmann, 'Capitalism, Patriarchy and Job Segregation by Sex', in Z. Eisenstein (ed) *Capitalist Patriarchy and the Case for Socialist Feminism*, Monthly Review Press, New York, 1979; Cynthia Cockburn, *Brothers*, Pluto Press, London, 1983.

30. Beatrix Campbell and Valerie Charlton, 'Work to Rule', 1978, reprinted in Feminist Anthology Collective, *No Turning Back*, The Women's Press, London, 1981; Angela Weir and Elizabeth Wilson, 'Towards a Wages Strategy for Women', *Feminist Review*, no.10, 1982.

31. Beatrix Campbell, *Wigan Pier Revisited*, Virago, London, 1984.

32. Sarah Benton, 'Needing a Feminist Voice', p.12, *New Statesman*, 22 March 1985.

33. 'The Women's Movement and the Labour Party: Interview with Labour Party Feminists', p.78, *Feminist Review*, no.16, 1984.

34. Interview with David Blunkett, in Martin Boddy and Colin Fudge (eds) *Local Socialism?*, p.255, Macmillan, London, 1984.

35. Sheila Lewenhak, *Women And Trade Unions*, p.161, Ernest Benn Ltd., London and Tunbridge, 1977.

36. *Women Workers 1975*, TUC, London, 1975.

37. *Women Workers 1972*, p.76, TUC, London, 1972.

38. These discussions are summarised in the annual report of the Women's Advisory Committee for 1975/76, *Women Workers 1976*, TUC, London, 1976.

39. *Women Workers 1973*, p.120, TUC, London, 1973.

40. Transcript of discussion at the 50th TUC Women's Conference, p.87, TUC library, London.

41. Kate Holman, *Spare Rib* 130, p.31, May 1983.

42. See for example Jenny Beale, *Getting It Together: Women as Trade Unionists*, Pluto Press, London, 1982.

43. Chris Joyce, *Working Class Women's Liberation Newsletter*, Summer 1979.

44. *WIRES*, no.23, November 1976.

45. Chris Joyce, *Working Class Women's Liberation Newsletter*, Summer 1979.

46. Evelyn Tension, 'You don't need a degree to read the writing on the

wall', p.10, London, 1979. (An abridged version was reprinted in Feminist Anthology Collective, *No Turning Back*, op.cit.)

47. ibid (1979 version) p.19.
48. 'I'm a Working Class Woman OK' p.15, *Spare Rib* 63, October 1977.
49. Marlene Packwood, 'The Colonel's Lady and Judy O'Grady: Class in the Women's Liberation Movement', p.10, *Trouble and Strife*, no.1, 1983.
50. John Carvel, *Citizen Ken*, p.202, Chatto and Windus, London, 1984.
51. 'Shirley, Wendy and Pat', *Spare Rib* 150, p.19, January 1985.
52. Tension, op.cit, p.15.
53. Packwood, op.cit., p.11.
54. 'Writing Our Own History: Interview with Wendy Collins, Al Garthwaite and Maria Spellacy, three of the first WIRES workers', pp. 54-55, *Trouble and Strife*, no.2, 1984.
55. See the questions posed by the Leeds Revolutionary Feminist Group for this conference: 'How is the term "sex class" used and abused? Does it gloss over economic class differences between women?' *WIRES*, no.74, 1979.
56. Quoted in Beverley Bryan, Stella Dadzie and Suzanne Scafe, *The Heart of the Race: Black Women's Lives in Britain*, p.174, Virago, London, 1985.
57. Sheila Rowbotham interviews Jean McCrindle, 'More than Just a Memory: Some Political Implications of Women's Involvement in the Miner's Strike 1984-85', p.113 *Feminist Review*, no.23, 1986.
58. ibid. p.117.
59. Quoted in Barnsley Women Against Pit Closures, *Women Against Pit Closures*, p.23, Barnsley, 1984.
60. McCrindle, op.cit, p.117.
61. Quoted in Liddington, op.cit, p.96.
62. Quoted in Liddington and Norris, op.cit. p.205.
63. McCrindle, op.cit, p.116.
64. Barnsley Women Against Pit Closures, *Women Against Pit Closures*, p.29, Barnsley, 1984.
65. Barnsley Women Against Pit Closures, *Women Against Pit Closures Vol II*, p.29, Barnsley, 1985.
66. Ann Harris, Nottinghamshire Women's Support Group, *Spare Rib* 151, p.6, February 1985.
67. Jacky Naylor, Nottinghamshire Women's Support Group, *Spare Rib*, 157, p.10, August 1985.
68. McCrindle, op.cit. p.121.

6   Out of Distortion: Into Confusion?

1. Sheila Jeffreys, *The Spinster and Her Enemies: Feminism and Sexuality 1880-1930*, p.154, Pandora, London, 1985.
2. Zoe Fairbairns, *Benefits*, Virago, London, 1979.
3. Zoe Fairbairns, 'On Writing *Benefits*', p.255., Feminist Anthology Collective (ed), *No Turning Back*, The Women's Press, London, 1981.
4. Fairbairns, *Benefits*, p.204.
5. Fairbairns, 'On Writing *Benefits*', p.258.
6. Michèle Barrett and Mary McIntosh, *The Anti-Social Family*, p.155, Verso, London, 1982.
7. Sheila Rowbotham, 'What Do Women Want? Woman-Centred Values and the World As It Is', p.51, *Feminist Review*, no.20, 1985.
8. Cynthia Cockburn, 'Trade Unions and the Radicalizing of Socialist Feminism', p.45, *Feminist Review*, no.16, 1984.
9. Amanda Sebestyen, 'Tendencies in the Movement: Then and Now', pp 20-21, *Feminist Practice: Notes From the Tenth Year!*, In Theory Press, London, 1979.
10. Ann Pettifor, 'Labour's Macho Tendency', p.39, *New Socialist*, No.30, September 1985.
11. For a recent expression of the way these debates have bred disagreements between women, see 'Feminism and Class Politics: a Round Table Discussion', *Feminist Review*, no.23, 1986. See also Anne Phillips, 'Class Warfare', *New Socialist*, no.23, February 1985.
12. Some of the arguments are summarised in Anne Phillips, *Hidden Hands: Women and Economic Policies*, Pluto Press, London, 1983.

Bibliography

Books and Pamphlets

N. Abercrombie and J. Urry, *Capital, Labour and the Middle Classes*, Allen and Unwin, London, 1983.

Ruth Adam, *A Woman's Place 1910-1975*, Chatto and Windus, London, 1975.

Michael Anderson, *Family Structure in Nineteenth Century Lancashire*, Cambridge University Press, Cambridge, 1971.

Mabel Atkinson, *The Economic Foundations of the Women's Movement*, Fabian Tract no.175, London, June 1914.

Olive Banks, *Faces of Feminism*, Martin Robertson, Oxford, 1981.

Barnsley Women Against Pit Closures, *Women Against Pit Closures*, Barnsley, 1984.

Barnsley Women, *Women Against Pit Closures: Vol 2*, Barnsley, 1985.

Michèle Barrett and Mary McIntosh, *The Anti-Social Family*, Verso, London, 1982.

Carol Bauer and Laurence Ritt (eds) *Free And Enobled*, Pergamon Press, Oxford, 1979.

Jenny Beale, *Getting It Together: Women as Trade Unionists*, Pluto Press, London, 1982.

Clementina Black (ed) *Married Women's Work*, Virago, London, 1983 (first published 1915).

Martin Boddy and Colin Fudge (eds) *Local Socialism?*, Macmillan, London, 1984.

Sarah Boston, *Women Workers and the Trade Unions*, Davis-Poynter, London, 1980.

David Bouchier, *The Feminist Challenge*, Macmillan, London, 1983.

Patricia Branca, *Silent Sisterhood: Middle Class Women in the Victorian Home*, Croom Helm, London, 1975.

Gail Braybon, *Women Workers in the First World War*, Croom Helm, London, 1981.

Beverley Bryan, Stella Dadzie and Suzanne Scafe, *The Heart of the Race: Black Women's Lives in Britain*, Virago, London, 1985.

Sandra Burman (ed) *Fit Work For Women*, Croom Helm, London, 1979.

Beatrix Campbell, *Wigan Pier Revisited*, Virago, London, 1984.

John Carvel, *Citizen Ken*, Chatto and Windus, London, 1984.

Ruth Cavendish, *Women On The Line*, Routledge and Kegan Paul, London, 1982.

Centre for Contemporay Cultural Studies, *The Empire Strikes Back: Race and Racism in 70s Britain*, Hutchinson, London, 1982.

J. Clarke, C. Critcher, R. Johnson (eds) *Working Class Culture*, Hutchinson University Library, London, 1979.

Cynthia Cockburn, *Brothers: Male Dominance and Technological Change*, Pluto Press, London, 1983.

Margaret Cole, *Women Of Today*, Book For Libraries Press, New York, 1968 (first published 1938).

Clara E. Collet, *The Economic Position of Educated Working Women*, South Place Ethical Society, London, 1890.

Anna Coote and Beatrix Campbell, *Sweet Freedom*, Pan, London, 1982.

Geoffrey Crossick (ed) *The Lower Middle Class in Britain 1870-1914*, Croom Helm, London, 1977.

James Curran (ed) *The Future of the Left*, Polity Press, Oxford, 1984.

Mary Daly, *Gyn/Ecology*, Beacon Press, Boston, 1978.

Angela Davis, *Women Race and Class*, The Women's Press, London, 1982.

Barbara Ehrenreich and Deirdre English, *For Her Own Good: 150 Years of the Experts' Advice to Women*, Pluto Press, London, 1979.

Zillah Eisenstein (ed) *Capitalist Patriarchy and the Case for Socialist Feminism*, Monthly Review Press, New York, 1979.

Zoe Fairbairns, *Benefits*, Virago, London, 1979.

Feminist Anthology Collective, *No Turning Back*, The Women's Press, London, 1981.

Feminist Practice: Notes From the Tenth Year!, In Theory Press, London, 1979.

Shulamith Firestone, *The Dialectic of Sex*, Jonathan Cape, London, 1971.

Formations of Pleasure Routledge and Kegan Paul, London, 1983.

John Foster, *Class Struggle and the Industrial Revolution*, Weidenfeld and Nicolson, London, 1974.

Jean Gaffin and David Thoms, *Caring and Sharing: The Centenary History of the Co-operative Women's Guild*, Co-operative Union Ltd, 1983.

Elizabeth Gaskell, *North and South*, Penguin, London, 1970 (first published 1854-5).

Anthony Giddens, *The Class Structure of the Advanced Societies*, Hutchinson, London, 1973.

Anthony Giddens and David Held (eds) *Classes, Power and Conflict*, Macmillan, London, 1982.

George Gissing, *The Odd Women*, London, 1893.

J.H. Goldthorpe with C. Llewellyn and C. Payne, *Social Mobility and Class Structure in Modern Britain*, Clarendon, Oxford, 1980.

A.H. Halsey, A.F. Heath and J.M. Ridge, *Origins and Destinations*, Clarendon Press, Oxford, 1980.

Margaret Hewitt, *Wives and Mothers in Victorian Industry*, Greenwood Press, Connecticut, 1974 (first published 1958).

May Hobbs, *Born To Struggle*, Quartet, London, 1973.

Lee Holcombe, *Victorian Ladies At Work*, David and Charles, London, 1973.

Lee Holcombe, *Wives and Property*, University of Toronto Press, Toronto, 1983.

Louisa M. Hubbard, *Work For Ladies in Elementary Schools*, London, 1872.

Inner London Education Authority, *Race, Sex and Class 1. Achievement in Schools*, ILEA, London, 1983.

Sheila Jeffreys, *The Spinster and Her Enemies: Feminism and Sexuality 1880-1930*, Pandora, London, 1985.

Angela V. John, *By the Sweat of Their Brow: Women Workers at Victorian Coal Mines*, Croom Helm, London, 1980.

Annette Kuhn and Ann Marie Wolpe (eds) *Feminism and Materialism*, Routledge and Kegan Paul, London, 1978.

Diana Leonard Barker and Sheila Allen (eds) *Dependence and Exploitation in Work and Marriage*, Longman, London, 1976.

Sheila Lewenhak, *Women And Trade Unions*, Ernest Benn Ltd., London and Tunbridge, 1977.

Jane Lewis, *Women In England 1870-1950*, Wheatsheaf, Sussex, 1984.

Jill Liddington, *The Life and Times of a Respectable Rebel: Selina Cooper 1864-1946*, Virago, London, 1984.

Jill Liddington and Jill Norris, *One Hand Tied Behind Us*, Virago, London, 1978

London Socialist Woman Group, *The Night-Cleaners' Campaign*, London, 1971.

Margaret Llewelyn Davies (ed) *Life As We Have Known It*, Virago, London, 1977, (first published 1931).

Margaret Llewelyn Davies (ed) *Maternity: Letters From Working Women*, Virago, London, 1978, (first published 1915).

Love Your Enemy?: The Debate Between Heterosexual Feminism and Political Lesbianism, OnlyWomen Press, London, 1981.

Ellen Mappen, *Helping Women At Work: The Women's Industrial Council 1889-1914*, Hutchinson/Explorations in Feminism Collective, London, 1985.

Jean Martin and Ceridwen Roberts, *Women And Employment: A Lifetime Perspective*, HMSO, London, 1984.

Betty Matthews (ed) *Marx: A Hundred Years On*, Lawrence and Wishart, London, 1983.

John Stuart Mill, *Three Essays*, Oxford University Press, London, 1975.

Kate Millett, *Sexual Politics*, Sphere, London, 1971.

J.D. Milne, *Industrial and Social Position of Women in the Middle and Lower Ranks*, London, 1857.

Hannah Mitchell, *The Hard Way Up*, Virago, London, 1977.

Juliet Mitchell, *Woman's Estate*, Penguin, London, 1971.

Juliet Mitchell and Ann Oakley (eds) *The Rights and Wrongs of Women*, Penguin, London, 1976.

Ann Oakley, *Housewife*, Allen Lane, London, 1974.

Frank Parkin, *Class Inequality and Political Order*, MacGibbon and Kee, London, 1977.

Maud Pember Reeves, *Round About A Pound A Week*, Virago, London, 1979, (first published 1913).

Anne Phillips, *Hidden Hands: Women and Economic Policies*, Pluto Press, London, 1983.

Ivy Pinchbeck, *Women Workers and the Industrial Revolution 1750-1850*, Virago, London, 1981, (first published 1930).

Christine de Pizan, *The Book of the City of Ladies*, Picador, London, 1983.

Anna Pollert, *Girls, Wives and Factory Lives*, Macmillan, London, 1981.

Marilyn Porter, *Home, Work and Class Consciousness*, Manchester University Press, Manchester, 1983.

The Power of Women and the Subversion of the Community, Falling Wall Press, London, 1972.

Marion Ramelson, *The Petticoat Rebellion*, Lawrence and Wishart, London, 1972.

Eleanor Rathbone, *The Disinherited Family*, Allen and Unwin, London, 1947.

Denise Riley, *War in the Nursery*, Virago, London, 1983.

Elizabeth Roberts, *A Woman's Place: An Oral History of Working-Class Women 1890-1940*, Basic Blackwell, Oxford, 1984.

Elizabeth Robins, *The Convert*, The Women's Press, London, 1980, (first published 1907).

A. Rosen, *Rise Up Women!*, Routledge and Kegan Paul, London, 1974.

Alice Rossi (ed) *J.S. Mill and Harriet Taylor Mill: Essays on Sex Equality*, University of Chicago Press, Chicago, 1970.

Sheila Rowbotham, *Woman's Consciousness, Man's World*, Penguin, London, 1973.

Sheila Rowbotham, Lynne Segal, Hilary Wainwright, *Beyond the Fragments*, London, 1979.

Sheila Rowbotham, *Dreams and Dilemmas*, Virago, London, 1983.

Dora Russell, *The Tamarisk Tree, Vol I*, Virago, London, 1977.

R. Samuel (ed) *Life and Labour*, Routledge and Kegan Paul, London, 1975.

Olive Schreiner, *Women and Labour*, Virago, London, 1978, (first published 1911).

Lynne Segal (ed), *What Is To Be Done About The Family?*, Penguin, London, 1983.

Sue Sharpe, *'Just Like A Girl': How Girls Learn to be Women*, Penguin, London, 1976.

Alix Kates Shulman, *Burning Questions*, Fontana, London, 1980.

Socialist Economic Review, Merlin, London, 1982.

Dale Spender, *Women of Ideas*, Routledge and Kegan Paul, London, 1982.

Ray Strachey, *The Cause*, Virago, London, 1978, (first published 1928).

Gareth Stedman Jones, *Languages of Class: Studies in English Working Class History 1832-1982*, Cambridge University Press, London, 1983.

Barbara Taylor, *Eve and the New Jerusalem*, Virago, London, 1983.

Evelyn Tension, *You don't need a degree to read the writing on the wall*, London, 1979.

E.P. Thompson, *The Making of the English Working Class*, Penguin, London, 1968.

Union of Women For Liberation, *On The Working Women's Charter*, London, 1975.

Lise Vogel, *Marxism and the Oppression of Women*, Pluto Press, London, 1983.

Martha Vicinus (ed) *A Widening Sphere: Changing Roles of Victorian Women*, Indiana University Press, Bloomington, 1977.

Christina Walkley, *The Ghost in the Looking Glass*, Peter Owen, London, 1981.

Judith Walkowitz, *Prostitution and Victorian Society: Women, Class and the State*, Cambridge University Press, London, 1980.

Jackie West (ed), *Work, Women and the Labour Market*, Routledge and Kegan Paul, London, 1982.

Sallie Westwood, *All Day Every Day*, Pluto Press, London, 1984.

Frances Widdowson, *Going Up Into The Next Class: Women and Elementary School Training*, Women's Research and Resources Centre Publications: Explorations in Feminism no 7, London, 1980.

Mary Wollstonecraft, *Vindication of the Rights of Woman*, Penguin, London, 1975, (first published 1792).

Virginia Woolf, *Women And Writing*, The Women's Press, London, 1979.

Articles in Journals or Books

Sally Alexander, 'Women's Work in Nineteenth Century London', in Juliet Mitchell and Ann Oakley (eds) *The Rights and Wrongs of Women*, Penguin, London, 1976.

Valerie Amos and Pratibha Parmar, 'Challenging Imperial Feminism', *Feminist Review*, no.17, 1984.

Michèle Barrett, 'Marxism-Feminism and the Work of Karl Marx', in Betty Matthews (ed) *Marx: A Hundred Years On*, Lawrence and Wishart, London, 1983.

Michèle Barrett and Mary McIntosh, 'The "Family Wage": Some Problems for Socialists and Feminists', *Capital and Class*, no.11, 1980.

Michèle Barrett and Mary McIntosh, 'Ethnocentrism and Socialist-Feminist Theory', *Feminist Review*, no.20, 1985.

R.D. Barron & G.M. Norris, 'Sexual Divisions and the Dual Labour Market' in Diana Leonard Barker and Sheila Allen (eds), *Dependence and Exploitation in Work and Marriage*, Longman, London 1976.

Veronica Beechey, 'Women and Production: a Critical Analysis of some Sociological Theories of Women's Work', in Annette Kuhn and Ann Marie Wolpe (eds), *Feminism and Materialism*, Routledge and Kegan Paul, London, 1978.

Sarah Benton, 'Needing a Feminist Voice', *New Statesman*, 22 March 1985.

Irene Bruegel, 'Women as a Reserve Army of Labour: a Note on Recent British Experience', *Feminist Review*, no.3, 1979.

Beatrix Campbell and Valerie Charlton, 'Work to Rule', 1978, reprinted in Feminist Anthology Collective, *No Turning Back*, The Women's Press, London, 1981.

Hazel Carby, 'White Women Listen! Black Feminism and the Boundaries of Sisterhood', in Centre for Contemporary Cultural Studies, *The Empire Strikes Back: Race and Racism in 70s Britain*, Hutchinson, London, 1982.

Cynthia Cockburn, 'Trade Unions and the Radicalizing of Socialist Feminism', *Feminist Review*, no.16, 1984.

Anna Coote, 'The AES: a New Starting Point', *New Socialist*, no.2, 1981.

Mariarosa Dalla Costa, 'Women and the Subversion of the Community', in *The Power of Women and the Subversion of the Community*, Falling Wall Press, London, 1972.

Leonore Davidoff, 'The Separation of Home From Work? Landladies and Lodgers in Nineteenth and Twentieth Century England', in Sandra Burman (ed) *Fit Work For Women*, Croom Helm, London, 1979.

'Ethnic Origin and Economic Status', *Employment Gazette*, Vol.91, No.10, October 1983.

Zoe Fairbairns, 'On Writing *Benefits*', Feminist Anthology Collective (ed), *No Turning Back*, The Women's Press, London, 1981.

'Feminism and Class Politics: a Round Table Discussion', *Feminist Review*, no.23, 1986.

Jean Gardiner and Sheila Smith, 'Feminism and the Alternative Economic Strategy', *Socialist Economic Review*, Merlin, London, 1982.

Elizabeth Garnsey, 'Women's Work and Theories of Class and Stratification' in A. Giddens and D. Held (eds), *Classes, Power and Conflict*, Macmillan, London, 1982.

John Goldthorpe, 'Women and Class Analysis: In Defence of the Conventional View', *Sociology*, 17.4, Nov. 1983.

Catherine Hakim, 'Sexual Division within the Labour Force: Occupational Segregation', *Employment Gazette*, November 1978.

Catherin Hakim, 'Job Segregation: Trends in the 1970s', *Employment Gazette*, December 1981.

Catherine Hall, 'The Early Formation of Victorian Domestic Ideology', in Sandra Burman (ed), *Fit Work For Women*, Croom Helm, London, 1979.

A. James Hammerton, 'Feminism and Female Emigration 1861-1886' in Martha Vicinus (ed), *A Widening Sphere: Changing Roles of Victorian Women*, Indiana University Press, Bloomington, 1977

Jalna Hanmer, Cathy Lunn, Sheila Jeffreys, Sandra McNeil, 'Sex-class: Why is it important to call women a class?', reprinted in *Scarlet Women* 5, 1977.

Heidi Hartmann, 'The Unhappy Marriage of Marxism and Feminism: Towards a More Progressive Union', *Capital and Class*, no.8, 1979.

Heidi Hartmann, 'Capitalism, Patriarchy and Job Segregation by Sex', in Z. Eisenstein (ed), *Capitalist Patriarchy and the Case for Socialist Feminism*, Monthly Review Press, New York, 1979.

Anthony Heath and Nicky Britten, 'Women's Jobs Do Make a Difference: A Reply to Goldthorpe', *Sociology*, 18.4, Nov. 1984.

Barbro Hoel, 'Contemporary Clothing "Sweatshops": Asian Female Labour and Collective Organisation', in Jackie West (ed), *Work, Women and the Labour Market*, Routledge and Kegan Paul, London, 1982.

Sheila Jeffreys, 'The Need for Revolutionary Feminism', reprinted in *Scarlet Women* 5, 1977.

Eva Kaluzynska, 'Wiping the Floor with Theory – a Survey of Writings on Housework', *Feminist Review*, no.6, 1980.

Cora Kaplan, 'Wild Nights', in *Formations of Pleasure*, Routledge Kegan Paul, London, 1983.

J. Kitteringham 'Country Work Girls in Nineteenth Century England' in R. Samuel (ed) *Life and Labour*, Routledge and Kegan Paul, London, 1975.

'Labour Force Survey: Preliminary Results for 1984', *Employment*

Gazette, Vol.93, No.5, May 1985.

Hilary Land, 'The Family Wage', *Feminist Review*, No.6, 1980.

Leeds Revolutionary Feminist Group, 'Political Lesbianism: The Case Against Heterosexuality', reprinted in *Love Your Enemy? The Debate Between Heterosexual Feminism and Political Lesbianism*, Only Women Press, London, 1981.

Frances Martin, 'A College For Working Women', in Carol Bauer and Laurence Ritt (eds), *Free And Enobled*, Pergamon Press, Oxford, 1979.

Jean McCrindle, 'More than Just a Memory: Some Political Implications of Women's Involvement in the Miners' Strike, 1984-1985', *Feminist Review*, no.23, 1986.

R. McWilliams-Tulberg, 'Women and Degrees at Cambridge University 1862-1897', in Martha Vicinus (ed), *A Widening Sphere: Changing Roles of Victorian Women*, Indiana University Press, Bloomington, 1977.

Juliet Mitchell, 'Women and Equality', in Juliet Mitchell and Ann Oakley (eds), *The Rights and Wrongs of Women*, Penguin, London, 1976.

Maxine Molyneux, 'Beyond the Domestic Labour Debate', *New Left Review*, no.116, 1979.

MORI poll 'Public Attitudes Towards Abortion', *Sunday Times*, January, 1980.

MORI poll 'Family Matters', *Sunday Times*, April, 1982.

Mica Nava, 'From Utopian to Scientific Feminism? Early Feminist Critiques of the Family', in Lynne Segal (ed), *What Is To Be Done About The Family?* Penguin, London, 1983.

Florence Nightingale, 'Cassandra', in Ray Strachey, *The Cause*, Virago, London, 1978.

Marlene Packwood, 'The Colonel's Lady and Judy O'Grady: Class in the Women's Liberation Movement', *Trouble and Strife*, no.1, 1983.

Bessie Rayner Parkes, 'The Market for Educated Female Labour', *The English Woman's Journal*, Nov.1859.

Bessie Rayner Parkes, 'What Can Educated Women Do?', *The English Woman's Journal*, Jan. 1860.

Ann Pettifor, 'Labour's Macho Tendency', *New Socialist*, no.30, September 1985.

Anne Phillips and Barbara Taylor, 'Sex and Skill: Notes Towards a Feminist Economics', *Feminist Review*, no.6, 1980.

Anne Phillips, 'Class Warfare', *New Socialist*, no.23, February 1985.

Annie Phizacklea, 'Migrant Women and Wage Labour: the Case of West Indian Women in Britain', in Jackie West (ed), *Work, Women and the Labour Market*, Routledge and Kegan Paul, London, 1982.

Caroline Rowan, 'Women in the Labour Party 1906-1920', *Feminist Review*, no.12, 1982.

Sheila Rowbotham, 'What Do Women Want? Woman-Centred Values

and the World As It Is', *Feminist Review*, no.20, 1985.

Amanda Sebestyen, 'Tendencies in the Movement: Then and Now', *Feminist Practice: Notes From the Tenth Year!*, In Theory Press, London, 1979.

Michelle Stanworth, 'Women and Class Analysis: a Reply to John Goldthorpe', *Sociology*, 18, 2, May 1984.

Barbara Taylor, ' "The Men are as Bad as Their Masters ..." Socialism, Feminism and Sexual Antagonism in the London Tailoring Trade in the Early 1830s', *Feminist Studies*, 5, no.1, 1979.

Pam Taylor, 'Daughters and Mothers – Maids and Mistresses: Domestic Service Between the Wars', in J. Clarke, C. Critcher, R. Johnson (eds), *Working Class Culture*, Hutchinson University Library, London, 1979.

Angela Weir and Elizabeth Wilson, 'Towards a Wages Strategy for Women', *Feminist Review*, no.10, 1982.

'The Women's Movement and the Labour Party: Interview with Labour Party Feminists', *Feminist Review*, no.16, 1984.

'Writing Our Own History: Interview with Wendy Collins, Al Garthwaite and Maria Spellacy, three of the first WIRES workers', *Trouble and Strife*, no.2, 1984.

Plus Miscellaneous articles/letters from:

Scarlet Women
Spare Rib
WIRES
Women's Newspaper
Women Workers: Report from the TUC Women's Conference
Working Class Women's Liberation Newsletter

Index

Is the Future Female?
Troubled Thoughts on Contemporary Feminism
LYNNE SEGAL

In one of the most provocative books for many years, Lynne Segal challenges many of the current feminist orthodoxies – on female sexuality, pornography, war and peace, psychoanalysis and sociobiology. She argues against the exponents – Mary Daly, Andrea Dworkin and Dale Spender among them – of the new apocalyptic feminism, which says that men wield power over women through terror, greed and violence and that only women, because of their essentially greater humanity, can save the world from social, ecological and nuclear disaster. She urges that to base the politics of feminism on innate and essential differences between men and women is mistaken, dangerous, and basically a counsel of despair, since its logical conclusion is that nothing can change. Things emphatically *have* changed for women, she asserts, and we must build on these changes, combining autonomy with alliances to alter power relations and forge a new future for women *and* men.

The Heart of the Race
Black Women's Lives in Britain
BEVERLEY BRYAN, STELLA DADZIE & SUZANNE SCAFE

'A balanced tribute to the undefeated creativity, resilience and resourcefulness of Black women in Britain today' – Margaret Busby, *New Society*

'A long overdue opportunity to set the record straight ... a considerable achievement' – Brenda Polan, *Guardian*

'Our aim has been to tell it as we know it, placing our story within its history at the heart of our race, and using our own voices and lives to document the day-to-day realities of Afro-Caribbean women in Britain over the past forty years.'

The Heart of the Race powerfully records what life is like for Black women in Britain: grandmothers drawn to the promise of the 'mother country' in the 1950s talk of a different reality; young girls describe how their aspirations at school are largely ignored; working women tell of their commitments to families, jobs, communities. With clarity and determination, these Afro-Caribbean women discuss their treatment by the Welfare State, their housing situations, their health, their self-images – and their confrontation with the racism they encounter all too often. Here too is Black women's celebration of their culture and their struggle to create a new social order in this country.

* *Winner of the Martin Luther King Memorial Prize 1985*

* *Chosen as one of the 20 selected titles for the Feminist Book Fortnight 1986*

Eve and the New Jerusalem
Socialism and Feminism in the Nineteenth Century
BARBARA TAYLOR

'Absolutely necessary reading as history and as a contribution to our contemporary understanding' – Raymond Williams, *Guardian*

'An eloquent history of Owenite feminism, drawing on a huge and richly varied store' – Marina Warner, *Sunday Times*

'The most important contribution to the history of the early utopian socialist movement made in the last decade' – J.F.C. Harrison

In the early nineteenth century, radicals in Europe and America began to conceive of a 'New Moral World', and struggled to create their own utopias, with collective family life, communal property, free love and birth control. In Britain, the Utopian Socialist Robert Owen attracted thousands of followers, many of them women, who for more than a quarter of a century attempted to put theory into practice in their local societies, in trade unions and in Communities of Mutual Association. Barbara Taylor's brilliant study of this visionary challenge opens the way to an important re-interpretation of the socialist tradition, and recovers the crucial connections between socialist aims and feminist aspirations.

One Hand Tied Behind Us

The Rise of the Women's Suffrage Movement

JILL LIDDINGTON and JILL NORRIS

The north of England was the cradle of the suffrage movement: here women worked long hours in factories and mills, struggled against poverty and hardship at home, and, at the turn of the century, fought not only for the vote but for a wide range of women's rights. These radical suffragists, amongst them remarkable women like Selina Cooper and Ada Nield Chew, called for equal pay, birth control and child allowances. They took their message to women at the factory gate and the cottage door, to the Co-operative Guilds and trade union branches. *One Hand Tied Behind Us*, using much unpublished material and interviews with the last surviving descendants of these suffragists, creates a vivid and moving portrait of strong women who, over seventy years ago, envisaged freedoms for which we are still fighting today.

'A brilliant and original contribution to the history of female suffrage' – *The Times*

Women in Trade Unions

BARBARA DRAKE

'With fascinating precision Barbara Drake details working women's wages and conditions within the context of an argument for equal pay and, ultimately, socialism. A must for afficionados of labour history' – *Good Book Guide*

'An invaluable work – the only detailed account of this topic in existence' – Jackie Barron, *Morning Star*

In this remarkable and influential work, produced by the Labour Research Department and the Fabian Women's Group in 1920, its author Barbara Drake, niece of Beatrice Webb, provides an impressively comprehensive study ranging from eighteenth-century 'combinations' to the First World War in which women became cheap 'substitute' labour. In a detailed survey of different industries and unions – amongst them, textile, printing, food and tobacco, and clerical work – she analyses the particular problems of women organizing in trade unions. *Women in Trade Unions* is much more than an impressive historical document for it presents to us issues which are still as relevant, still as crucial to the future of women in the eighties as they were in the 1920s.

Married Women's Work

Edited by CLEMENTINA BLACK

The survey, made between 1909 and 1910 by the Women's Industrial Council, looked at the 'crying evil' of low wages and at women's burden of 'combined household and industrial toil far too heavy for any creature.' Fired by the conviction that substantial knowledge was needed to get public support for legislative reform, the investigators looked at the vast range of work done by married women and widows in all the major cities and many rural areas of Britain. In fascinating detail, we learn about the work conditions and home life of mantle makers, rag pickers, charwomen, weavers, fruit pickers, shopkeepers, hawkers – and many, many more.

Out of print since 1915, this is a formidable source book for historians, and contributes, with all-too-much relevance, to the unresolved debates around women, work and the family. But it is more than this: like its famous companion volume, *Round About a Pound a Week*, it is a marvellously rich portrait of the daily lives of working people, and their endurance in the face of overwork, ill health and poverty.

Independent Women
Work and Community for Single Women 1850-1920
MARTHA VICINUS

'Real life was hardly less passionate than fiction, nor less poignant, as Professor Vicinus's study of women in church communities, hospitals, colleges, boarding schools, and 'settlement houses' among the poor, amply and compellingly reveals' – Antonia Fraser, *The Guardian*

In mid-nineteenth century England, the Ideal Woman was the devoted wife and mother. But what of those thousands of single middle-class women who were described as 'superfluous'? In this remarkable and original study, the well-known historian Martha Vicinus examines the lives and ambitions, work and communities of this 'new species of womanhood'. Amongst their concerns, they sought to open new professions to women, improve education, and to assert women's political and economic rights. Residential houses and religious sisterhoods, women's colleges and boarding-schools, hospital nursing and social work settlements with their vision of community life for working-class girls and women – all these became their domain. Within half a century, they had carved out a special sphere for themselves which was neither that of the old maid, nor of the mother, nor of the dishonoured prostitute. Publicly and passionately they asserted their new-found power, not only through their demand for the vote, but for the reform of the whole of society and women's place in it.

Dreams and Dilemmas
Collected Writings
SHEILA ROWBOTHAM

'How do we hand on more than the outer husks of history? We were only dimly conscious of embarking on a historical process. The intensity, the need to talk, to be with other women, the discovery of self in a new relationship with others, the opening of understanding, the strength of trust and the mutuality of communication were immediate delights. They left marks and are too valuable to be forgotten'.

Sheila Rowbotham is one of the most original feminist thinkers of the past decade. She is also a prolific writer, and this collection, bringing together work from the late 1960s to the present day, offers a wonderfully detailed and thoughtful record of the contemporary women's movement, and its relationship to socialism – a subject particularly close to her heart.

The pieces range widely, and the collection includes previously unpublished material and poetry. Sheila Rowbotham writes about the first stirrings of the movement, about sexuality, race, housework, the welfare state, political organisation, trade unions, children, religion, history, books, and much else.

But people and movements change; we are now in the 1980s, and Sheila Rowbotham has added new introductions and linking passages which provide not only a fascinating commentary on her writings but a provocative re-evaluation of events and ideas from the recent past. The result is a timely and passionate plea for a renewal of feminism and socialism.

Sexuality
A Reader
Edited by FEMINIST REVIEW

The debate around sexuality which, in recent years, has opened up important areas of understanding and division among women, remains one of the most keenly felt and vociferously argued in the feminist arena. This collection of seventeen articles from the journal *Feminist Review* brings together some of the major contributions to that debate since the late seventies, both from Britain and the United States. Wide-ranging in its perspective, the book includes discussion of issues relating to sexual politics, the social construction of femininity and masculinity, psychoanalysis, lesbianism, pornography and representation, sexual violence and adolescence. Among the contributors are Beatrix Campbell, Rosalind Coward, Toril Moi, Elizabeth Wilson and, from America, Ellen DuBois, Deirdre English and Ruby Rich.

Waged Work
A Reader
Edited by FEMINIST REVIEW

The changing role of women in paid employment has been a central issue in feminist debate since the 1970s. This collection of key articles from the influential *Feminist Review* presents major contributions to that debate, reflecting both the scope and significance of work in the lives of women and the questions yet to be addressed by society at large. Wide-ranging and provocative, the articles look at the concepts of 'skill' and 'the reserve army of labour', and discuss the weaknesses of equal opportunities' legislation, the impact of privatisation and new technology, and the place of women – and feminism – in the trade union movement. They examine the question of whether a woman's earning her own income helps redress the balance of power between men and women, the role of women in Third World manufacturing, and the issues raised by recent anti-racist work in Britain.